Laws, Regulations, and Standards Governing Information in Cloud and Personal Computers

First Printing: 2017

ISBN-10:0-9985040-2-5
ISBN-13:978-0-9985040-2-5

Validated Quality Systems Publishing
1275 Bridle Path Dr
Lansdale PA 19446

www.validatedqualitysystems.com
www.vqsstaffing.com
www.sionaddtechnologies.com

Laws, Regulations, and Standards Governing Information in Cloud and Personal Computers

Darral Addison

Validated Quality Systems Publishing

2017

Table of Contents

Preface

If you use a computer for managing information then, I strongly suggest you read this book. You need to know what laws and regulations governing agencies have put in place to protect personal, private, and confidential information in your cloud, personal computer system, and compute devices.

For every piece of data, floating around in cyberspace a computer system has been developed to interpret the data, verify its legitimacy, protect its interest, and maintain its existence. Regulatory Agencies have created a set of expectations for companies who develop and operate computer systems in regulated spaces. It does not matter if your device is in a doctor's office, a server in an IT department, equipment on the manufacturing floor, automation in a business office or a cloud system managed by a third party offshore, you need to know what these agencies want from you and your computer system.

Information creation, maintenance, and security are key contributors driving the steadily growing information marketplace. The more critical information we are exposed to, the more secure we see ourselves and the more confident we are about our decisions. We believe our self-image and the health of our business is related to the amount of essential information we have at our disposal. What we do not understand is that, if we neglect the rules for creating, protecting and maintaining information our growth could be eaten up in legal fees, government fines, levies and jail time.

There is no shortage of information in the world. Volumes of legislation are being created every year to ensure that information is representative of the facts, free from misinterpretation, and falsification. Regulatory bodies use the same legislation to create healthy industry practices to promote good behavior for companies who are in the business of generating information.

Very few people are aware that, computing technology design, development, testing, and maintenance are governed by laws, regulations, guidance, standards and funding priorities. You need to know the legislative spirit behind the enforcement of the regulations, policies, codes, rules, and standards governing personal, private, and confidential information in the cloud, personal computer, and compute devices. It is critical that we understand how these laws and regulations apply because; they provide the blueprints for building a system that will pass regulatory scrutiny.

This book will make plain how governmental agencies promulgate policies that aid in the acceptance of Cloud and Computerized systems and It will help you understand how the mismanagement of personal, private and confidential information in corporations and small offices could lead to court disputes, penalties, debarment, and imprisonment.

Chapter 1

Cloud Acceptance

Computing Evolution

Some see cloud computing as a new phenomenon. Cloud computing is not a new phenomenon, but it is a constantly evolving paradigm. Cloud computing has its beginnings in parallel, grid, and utility computing. Parallel and grid computing are the ancient forerunners to the cloud computing model. Grid and parallel computing provide a strong historical insight into the ways in which IT and compute muscle have evolved. For the most part, each evolving paradigm is invisible to the average person but has made tremendous contributions to our way of life.

Parallel computing consists of the simultaneous use of multiple computer or computing resources to solve computational problems. In this paradigm, multiple processors operate concurrently to solve problems. The problem is broken down into discrete parts and solved simultaneously by different processors. Parallel computing requires a lot of energy, control, and coordination between the various central processing units. 1

The migration from parallel to grid computing is more about the where than the how. Grid computing is spread out over multiple locations. Grid computing requires processing coordination between various computers.2 Grid computing builds upon the parallel computing paradigm by allowing individual systems to contribute to the compute muscle for solving problems. Grid computing allows scientists, developers, and administrators to take advantage of simultaneous processing over considerable distances. Grid computing leverages the resources of multiple systems to crunch out data. In this paradigm, hundreds of computers are linked together in a matrixed like formation similar to that of a grid. The network can utilize or build upon each system's processing power to solve a problem. Grid computing systems can be as simple as a collection of similar computers running mathematical and academic problems or as complex as inter-networked systems utilized for drug discovery, seismic analysis, or economic forecasting. Each system plays a particular role in solving the problem. Grid computing gave rise to a new paradigm called

---

[1] (Matloff, 2015)

[2] (Joseph, Fellenstein, and Moss, 2003)

utility computing, where computer resources have the ability to be metered out as a service. 3

"I value order above all."

Utility computing is another computing paradigm shift. Unlike grid computing, the utility computing model has moved capacity to solve problems from individual workstations to shared servers which are available through web browsers rather than personal computers. Utility computing allows users to have access to a wide range of multiple computer resources and services via the Internet. This is achieved at heightened speeds, and fast computational abilities, by sharing resources. You can link to your neighbor's server or local computer to retrieve or save

[3] (Lutchman, 2003)

files. In essence, you are sharing their resources. The best thing about these services is that they can be metered out. Utility computing allows entities to share applications online. Applications can be pushed out to your computer as a service online as needed. Companies can go online and push out resources and free up hard drive space, operating systems updates, and applications for less than it would cost to buy at a computer store. Administrators could whisk information to any location around the globe for archiving, backup, or general storage. The best thing about this new paradigm is that these services are always available as long as the grid is up. You would no longer have to get in your car and drive to the local computer store to buy an email application or use the postal service to mail out an application on a CD-ROM for patches and fixes. You can just log in online to any conventional browser and download the applications or push out the fixes. With the power behind utility computing, no one thought that life could get better.

Eventually, utility computing migrated from the laboratories, system administrators, and back-end processing for managing orders, inventory, and supply chain into the public sector. Utility computing evolved into cloud computing. Like utility computing, cloud computing is the ultimate share community where network-based subscriptions and applications are shared globally. The difference is that cloud computing migrated into being sold as a service. Services such as online music and movie streaming, online banking, educational, social networking services, and web-based emails are delivered metered out and marketed as a service to subscribers around the world.

Cloud computing is truly a global phenomenon. Not only can applications, software services, and storage resources be leveraged as an external or internal resource from your virtual office but they can also be accessed from anyplace in the world where there is network access. Services can be bought and sold to the general public. Big companies and environments that require high processing speeds, more hard drive storage, and bandwidth can lease these resources externally from service providers without having to invest in their existing infrastructure. Small companies can purchase business software packages to build a virtual office online without ever having to leave their living room. The cloud paradigm has opened up opportunities for various service providers to profit from the changing paradigm. Brokers, cloud service providers (CSPs), platform service providers (PSP), infrastructure providers, application service providers (ASPs), etc., and software development companies are just a few entities in a stream of solution providers working towards allowing businesses, consumers, and governments the ability to benefit from cloud computing. Purchasing software in the cloud eliminates the need for each entity (person, organization or business) to buy cumbersome hardware, mortar and brick locations, or unconfigurable software for their IT infrastructure. As long as each entity maintains their commitment to sharing or metering their resources, everyone can benefit. The cloud is only as good as each contributor.

Cloud computing technology not only gives you the ability to download applications and get access to information, but you can also leverage pay-as-you-go services. Most companies will allow you to pay for the services you need instead of having to sign a long-term contract or to commit to services you will seldom use. In the past, if you needed to increase your hard drive capacity you would back up your information, open up your computer and install your new drive or take your computer to the computer service center to install a new hard disk. Well, in the cloud paradigm, you only go online, find a company who will lease you their storage space and use the new location as an extended drive. Cloud computing gives users the ability to meter out compute power, data storage, bandwidth usage, and more. The result of combining technology resources yields decreased IT infrastructure. Cloud computing will allow you to minimize your IT infrastructure by outsourcing your need for more compute power, data storage, bandwidth usage, etc. Even though a portion of your network will be leveraged offsite, you can purchase pay-as-you-go security services online to ensure that only you can access your information. Cloud computing provides increased accessibility and availability of cloud resources. You can store information in the cloud, and retrieve it on-demand. Cloud computing has become the marvel of the world. As expected, cloud computing has emerged as one of the most powerful archetypes to date.

Cloud Space

Cloud computing has been described as a unique scalable architecture. While it is true that the information in the cloud rides on top of an underlying architecture, no one design defines the cloud. How the Cloud is structured is inconsequential. It does not matter if the architecture is expanded upon, redesigned or open to the public because the paradigm's existence is predicated upon the fact that you can combine different designs. The life of the cloud is based upon the assimilation of various structures to consume information.

Try not to look at cloud computing as just a collection of software and chip components. Also, do not consider it as a central entity that manages services and is controlling traffic and access from a central office. When cloud computing is referenced, it is a reference to everyone who takes part in services and activities in the infinite space. The cloud is not defined by schematics found in the hardware or software drawings. The cloud is a virtual community that comes to life. Cloud computing is a fluid paradigm. You can enter the cloud in many different ways. Everyone who willingly or unwillingly contributes information to the paradigm brings it to life. Everyone who has an electronic device adds to the cloud's existence. Bits and pieces of information that define who you are may reside in some entity's cloud. The cloud is an anomaly. It's defined by millions of people's desire to pull together resources and search for information.

Service Providers

Always remember that the cloud is a virtual community. Any one of the below entities can provide access to services to the cloud. You can enter the cloud in many different ways (laptop, telephone, cell phone, PDA, iPad, smartphones and tablet computers, wearable computers, smart watches, game consoles, portable media players, and more. Everyone who willingly or unwillingly contributes information to the paradigm brings the cloud to life. These contributions and solutions are available on demand. Anyone can subscribe to practically any service almost anywhere in the world.

Internet Service Provider (ISP)

Individuals and companies turn to an ISP when they need to have an Internet connection to access services in the cloud. From the Internet, you will get immediate access to thousands of applications and services such as online music and movies streaming, online banking, taxes, educational, social networking services, and web-based email. You can also get access to computing power, data storage, and bandwidth usage in the form of pay-as-you-go services.

Cloud Service Provider (CSP)

For companies that do not have the capital and expertise to build their cloud or that would like to utilize the services of a cloud supplier for infrastructure, or application services, they can purchase services from the CSP. CSPs are companies that offer dedicated and secure cloud infrastructure, or application services. These services are hosted in a data center that can be accessed over the Internet. Most service providers offer customers controlled and managed data center space with numerous connectivity options to house computing, storage, telecom and application server equipment. Depending on customer requirements, open racks, cabinets, or customized caged floor spaces are available across a global footprint of secure facilities. These facilities are designed to withstand major environmental incidents. 4

There is a plethora of service infrastructure supporting cloud activities. When we refer to these services, we use the xSP (ISP, ASP, MSP, HSP, SSP, WSP, NSP, etc.) service infrastructure acronym. Some of the service providers (SPs) by which we access the cloud include but are not limited to:

- Internet Service Provider (ISP): Provides users with connection to the Internet
- Network Service Provider (NSP): Business or organization that sells bandwidth or network access by providing direct Internet backbone access to the Internet and usually access to its network access points
- Cloud Service Provider (CSP): A service provider that offers customers storage or software services available in the cloud
- Application Service Provider (ASP): Provides remote access to one or more computer applications
- Storage Service Provider (SSP): A company that provides computer storage space and related management to services
- Virtual IT Service Provider (VISP): Provides virtual services such as monitoring, reporting, remote management, backups, security and updates from a remote location

An ISP allows the customer to take advantage of online music and movie streaming. The CSP allows businesses to make use of Infrastructure as a Service (IaaS). IaaS allows equipment used to support your operations, such as storage, hardware, servers, and networking components, to be

[4] (Metheny, 2013)

leased from a CSP. Likewise, Software as a Service (SaaS) allows users to take advantage of applications that are designed and hosted by software vendors around the globe and made available over the Internet. Platform as a Service (Paas) offers entities working on computer based development projects an excellent opportunity to work in a dedicated environment that can easily be leased by entities that need a virtual workspace. Whether you need a dedicated research or a stable and secure environment, numerous options can cater to your needs. Cloud computing is incredibly nimble. Consumers can jump, slip or slide into the fun. Moving into on-demand cloud services through mobile devices, smartphones, personal digital assistants, manifests, tablets, and various services in the cloud is a cinch. You can work anywhere because the cloud works everywhere.

"We're going to shrink your department even more."

US Government Computing Initiative

The Office of Management and Budget (OBM) chartered the Infrastructure Optimization Initiative (IOI) in 2006. The goal of the (IOI) is to develop strategic infrastructure initiatives to operate and maintain IT infrastructure efficiently and effectively. The IOI helps government agencies understand the underlying performance metrics when determining the effectiveness of particular services being offered by service providers. IOI wanted to compile and post the parameters in a central location so that government agencies can pick various services that are aligned with their mission. These metrics will help them achieve optimum performance. Performance metrics such as response time, peak capacity, throughput, demand management, availability, and downtime are just some of IOI performance metrics needing more clarity.

The performance level metrics were packed as a set of expectations for government agencies when entering into an agreement with a service provider. Before a government agency enters into a service level agreement (SLA) with a service provider, they could refer to the performance metrics as a gauge or a standard set of level service expectations for determining the reliability of the Service Provider. These service level expectations were packaged into what is now called Best Practices. IOI Best Practices define the set of performance standards expected to be used by governmental agencies when searching for a reliable service provider. Best Practices chronicles the level of the quality of service as well as the range of services of all of the parties in the service level agreement. It also defines the way that services are to be rendered and prioritized. According to IOI, the SLA defines relationships and sets expectations by describing the availability and delivery of services. If the levels of services are inadequate, compromised or if they cannot be rendered, the SLA can be referenced for mitigating contract disputes.

As new technology comes on line requiring new performance metrics, so will the need for redefining performance metrics in the SLA. The SLA must be crafted in such a static way even though standards are always changing. SLAs may have multiple stakeholders and therefore will not look alike. The SLA's existence is dependent on the types of services and products delivered over time. The multi-layer SLAs may include commitments with the service provider who has an agreement with the platform provider, who has an agreement with the infrastructure provider, who has an agreement with the application provider, who has an agreement with the software development company. IOI is responsible for optimizing government IT resources so that government agencies can focus on their mission priorities and not have to question if their CSP is providing them with a stable and reliable service.

IOI was later designated as the IT Infrastructure Line of Business (ITILOB).5 ITILOB's goal is to use a cloud computing technology platform that includes optimization strategies, performance metrics, and infrastructure tools for benchmarking federal IT data. In other words, ITILOB was assigned the responsibility to create an optimized, cost-effective collaborative Federal Government framework for all federal

[5] (*Exhibit 300 Capital Asset Plan And Business Case Summary*)

agencies. ITILOB spearheaded a government-wide study of end user systems and support, telecommunications, mainframe and server services. ITILOB established some expectations for cloud computing services. The result of the study was a written report. The report focused on encouraging the optimization, performance, efficiency, and effectiveness of the Federal Government's IT services. The report was so impactful that the Federal Chief Information Officer (CIO) Council identified cloud computing as a Federal IT priority. The CIO found it strategically necessary to form a CIO working group called Cloud Computing Executive Steering Committee (CCESC). 6

CCESC was established in March of 2009. CCESC estimated that over twenty billion of the Federal Government's eighty billion IT spending budget is a potential target for migration to cloud computing solutions.

CCESC's initiative is to drive innovation and encourage public partnerships that will foster the realization of a cloud computing

[6] (Schlosser et al., 2009)

framework. The upfront cost associated with the consolidation of IT resources is enormous. However, it is believed that the Federal Government can save as much as twenty billion dollars by utilizing a cloud platform. Twenty billion dollars is a staggering amount of money. The savings associated with re-engineering an architecture, migrating data, and streamlining applications is a game changer. CCESC wanted to transfer operating complexities that once were in the domain of administrators to be integrated into an automated framework that's outside the periphery of the users. The result will be a decreased infrastructure and an increased availability of on-demand cloud services. CCESC is comprised of four subgroups:

1. The Communications Subgroup is responsible for communicating the state of cloud computing within the Federal Government to federal agencies. It is responsible for conveying the cloud's functions and the purposes behind the functions.
2. The Operational Excellence Subgroup is responsible for providing assistance to federal agencies concerning cloud computing. It determines if the specifics within cloud computing have the potential of fitting into various agencies' operating framework and tries to uncover potential applications for cloud computing, and possible improvements.
3. The Standards Subgroup is responsible for developing standards and policies that will ensure that diverse systems and organizations can integrate procedures without negative consequences and ensure that the moving of data between cloud providers, whether public or private is accomplished with ease.
4. The Security Subgroup is responsible for ensuring that the cloud environment is secure. It ensures that security standards and controls are in place for housing data in the cloud.

In 2013, the Federal Government had over seven thousand data centers.7 In February 2010, the Federal Data Center Consolidation Initiative

(FDCCI) was launched. The goal of FDCCI was to develop standards and policies, detailed consolidation plans, and technical roadmaps to eliminate no less than 800 federal data centers by 2015. This effort was to centralize the hosting of key applications and eliminate the need for infrastructure components that had become redundant. Ultimately, the effort reduced complexity within the federal IT environment.

In 2011, the CIO was responsible for creating a Strategic Information Resource Management Plan for the federal government. The plan was centered on resourcing information and technology management activities for cloud computing to federal agencies. The CIO was responsible for ensuring that the federal agencies' movement to the cloud was adequately funded and in alignment with each agency's business strategy. The goal of this plan was to have each federal agency evaluate its current technology to see if cloud computing was a viable option. Federal agencies were tasked to investigate the benefits of cloud computing, develop a path and framework for establishing cloud computing, and apply resources for and develop roles and responsibilities to support cloud-based initiatives. Federal agencies were expected to investigate and invest in cloud computing technologies and adopt solutions that were cost-effective, reliable, and easy to integrate.

It's no secret that the CIO was well aware that operational efficiencies, for cloud computing communities, exceed the unnecessary cumbersome energy gulping data centers. Cloud computing communities are extremely elastic and have the potential to pool and reuse resources.

---

[7] (S. Rept. 113-157 - The Federal Data Center Consolidation Act of 2013)

Each community can achieve numerous deployment options that can make federal IT frameworks extremely agile and elastic while at the same time experience substantial reductions in cost. The cloud computing initiative is centered on providing a broad range of federal agencies' immediate access to scale up utilizing virtualized hardware and/or software infrastructure. Each agency will have computing resources at its disposal for achieving unparalleled scalability by design.

Most CSPs provide a suite of services from colocation to fully managed hosting. These services should include Privacy Level Agreements (PLAs) and SLAs from hardware to applications. CSPs provide an unlimited number of different services.

The General Services Administration (GSA) is an influential participant in the Federal Cloud Computing Initiative (FCCI).8 GSA is a key player in implementing projects and planning activities for the acquisition, deployment and utilization of cloud computing technology. The objective of the FCCI is to make cloud-computing services accessible and easy to procure for federal agencies. FCCI is also working towards increasing operational efficiencies, and program optimization between government agencies. Obscuring IT boundaries between federal agencies and realizing increased collaboration and data centralization within the Federal Government is a primary goal. The FCCI facilitated one of the first initiatives to create the Federal Government's definition of cloud computing.

---

[8] (KellyJOlson, 2011)

The FCCI Executive Steering Committee, Advisory Council, and Working Groups are constantly working on identifying and addressing issues and obstacles to successful cloud computing implementation. FCCI's Executive Steering Committee's cloud computing mission statement is to reinforce, encourage, and expand the government-wide adoption of cost effective, green, and sustainable Federal cloud computing solutions. They are working towards establishing secure, easy to use, rapidly provisioned cloud IT services. These services include but are not limited to:

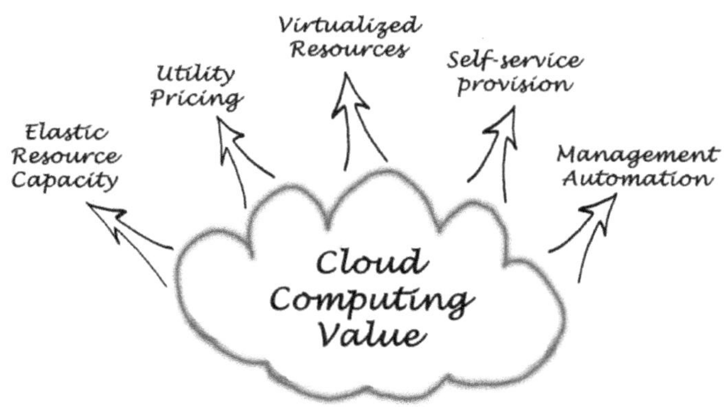

1. Developing a fast but yet simple acquisition and certification processes for cloud computing technology
2. Ensuring elasticity and smooth integration usage-based delivery of pooled computing resources
3. Ensuring business solutions are reusable and interoperable
4. Providing browser-based ubiquitous Internet access to services are accessible, always on and available

The GSA, the Department of Defense (DoD), the Department of Homeland Security (DHS), the National Institute of Standards and Technology (NIST), the OMB, and others work together to create the Federal Risk and Authorization Management Program (FedRAMP). 9 FedRAMP's goal is to ensure secure cloud systems. This program includes a government-wide, standardized approach to security assessments and ongoing continuous monitoring and authorizations of CSPs. FedRAMP works closely with cyber security and cloud experts from the NIST, GSA, DHS, DoD, NSA, and OMB to develop and implement security requirements for the Federal agency cloud-computing environment.10

1. NIST will lead and collaborate with federal, state, and local government agency CIOs, private-sector experts, and international bodies to identify and prioritize cloud computing standards and guidance
2. GSA will develop government-wide procurement vehicles and develop government-wide and cloud-based application solutions where needed
3. DHS will monitor operational security issues related to the cloud
4. DoD will accept and integrate a standardized approach to security assessments, authorizations and continuous monitoring for cloud products and services from FedRAMP.
5. The NSA will be responsible for evaluating their sourcing strategies to consider cloud computing solutions fully
6. Federal CIO Council will drive government-wide adoption of the cloud, identify next-generation cloud technologies, and share best practices and reusable example analyses and templates

---

[9] (Program overview, no date)

[10] (Department of Homeland Security, Office of the Chief Procurement Officer, 2015)

7. The OMB will coordinate activities across governance bodies, set overall cloud-related priorities, and guide agencies

The monitoring and authorization of CSPs save cost, time, and staff resources for federal agencies. It allows a one-time upfront assessment. The results of the evaluation are made available to all government institutions and businesses. A CSP's involvement in the standards program is optional. Any cloud service provider can apply to FedRAMP to be assessed. Once the assessment is completed, the CSP's quality of service, security controls, and security plan are published throughout the federal community. FedRAMP oversees the security testing that is conducted through a third party. If the CSP passes the assessment, FedRAMP makes a risk-based decision to determine whether to grant provisional authorization. Once permission is granted, federal agencies can petition FedRAMP for CSPs who are capable of meeting the requirements contained in the SLA, PLA, application-level, etc. Federal agencies can search FedRAMP to see if the providers' security credentials uphold risk clearance for hosting electronic data. Once authorization is granted, the CSP can be solicited for their services. The CSP is subject to ongoing security assessments.

NIST

NIST provides technical leadership for the nation's measurement and standards infrastructure for measurement phenomena. The Information Technology Laboratory (ITL) is one of the major research organizations within NIST.11 ITL acknowledges the immense short-term and long-term benefits by investing in cloud infrastructure. One of ITL's broader initiatives is to understand and define measurement phenomenon for science, technology, mathematics, and statistics. ITL develops test methods, reference data, proof of concept implementations, and technical analysis to advance the development and productive use of information technology. Additional responsibilities include the development of technical, physical, administrative, and management standards and guidelines for the cost-effective security and privacy of sensitive

[11] (Hawes, 2016)

unclassified information in the federal computing community. ITL's goal is to develop cost-effective guidelines that make financial sense, and that can be integrated or woven into the global IT fabric. The Computer Security Division of ITL, NIST, developed the definition of cloud computing. NIST's Special Publication defines cloud computing in very distinct terms.

> *Cloud Computing is a model for enabling convenient, on-demand network access to a shared pool of configurable computing resources (e.g., networks, servers, storage, applications, and services) that can be rapidly provisioned and released with minimal management effort or service provider interaction. This cloud model promotes availability and is composed of five essential characteristics, three service models, and four deployment models.*

Cloud technology is constantly evolving. The above definition is not designed to put cloud computing expectations in a box where the potential new paradigm must conform. The NIST definition merely serves as a baseline for gauging cloud services and deployment models. It is probably better to think of it as an explanation than an expectation. Cloud computing is not an out-of-the-box solution. Cloud computing technology is a trial and error process or a grand experiment. It is a risk-based experiment where the stakeholders map out how information will be collected, encrypted, and sent around the world.

Infrastructure needs may not necessarily be mapped out in a guideline or provided as an architectural realization that is defined in a book but may be a unique cloud hybrid that is aligned with your business goals. Take time to develop an assessment to find out what is expected from the cloud or how goals will be achieved. It is important that you experiment with various cloud deployment models to ensure that you have the right services and characteristics that suit your business objectives.

Essential Cloud Characteristics

CSPs are making numerous claims about the benefits of adopting cloud technology. Some of the claims can be easily seen, but for others, the benefits are not readily visible. For example, while many companies are experiencing tremendous savings in infrastructure reductions and an increase of on-demand products and services, others are hiring new staff to integrate their existing platform into the cloud fabric. What is good for the goose may not be good for the gander. Nevertheless, some of the most common benefits of cloud computing technology are that it provides access to a broader audience and pools computational muscle, bandwidth, and processing speed in a seamless fashion. Cloud computing technology must have something distinctive that makes it unique and identifiable. NIST strongly suggests that the phrase "cloud computing" be reserved but not limited to systems that have five essential characteristics. 12

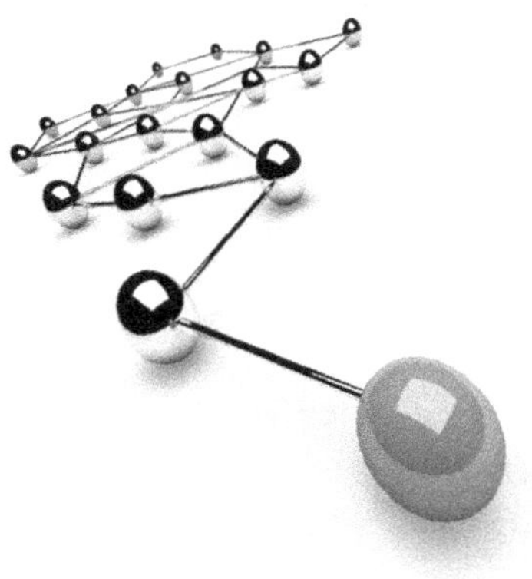

1. Scalable: It must be a flexible, scalable solution that can be scaled up or down, at any time.
2. Accessible: It must host ubiquitously available devices such as smartphones, personal data assistants, and various other computing platforms, and allow you to access your information from anywhere, and on any device.
3. Rapid Elasticity: Resources can be added to a network through the cloud without having to install and configure tests and validate additional servers.
4. Resource Driven: Computing resources can be pooled into a single location to serve all consumers using a multi-tenant model that can be dynamically assigned and reassigned on demand. The exact location of the provided resources need not be revealed.

---

[12] (Mell and Grance, 2012)

5. Metered: A measured service for which you pay per use as resources are needed.

Service Models

Cloud computing technology can conform to many different service models delivering a plethora of services. Cloud computing can be configured to provide many different types of services. These models include but are not limited to:

1. SaaS – Software as a Service: A delivery model in which software is provided and licensed across the Internet on a subscription basis and is centrally hosted and typically accessed by users using a device via a web browser.
2. PaaS – Platform as a Service: Is a model where customers can work online to develop, execute, and manage applications for launching an application.
3. IaaS – Infrastructure as a Service: Is the provisioning, processing, storage, and building of networks, and other virtualized computing resources over the Internet where the user has control over operating systems, storage, and applications and can run arbitrary software, but has limited control over the underlying cloud physical infrastructure.
4. StaaS – Storage as a Service: Is a service model in which a service provider provides digital storage on their own infrastructure in which space is rented on a subscription basis over the Internet.
5. TaaS – Testing as a Service: Is the outsourcing of an area of testing to a service provider. Usually, this includes non-critical automated regression testing, performance testing, security testing, testing of software, and cloud-based applications.
6. SecaaS – Security as a Service: Involves the deployment of security applications such as anti-virus, logging, authentication, single sign-on, authorization, device profiling, encryption, alerting, malware detection/prevention over the Internet by an outside organization.
7. DaaS – Desktop as a Service: Is a virtual desktop infrastructure (VDI) in which the customer's personal data is copied to and from

a virtual desktop that is independent of the user's location, device, and network. The VDI is managed by a third party who administers the back-end infrastructure.

8. MaaS – Monitoring/Management as a Service: Is a collection of information technology tools for gathering information regarding the applications and hardware operating at the client's location as well as supply activity reports. Monitoring provides remote tracking of network and computer health and to enhance the overall performance and management of the resources.
9. CaaS – Communication, Content, and Computing as a Service: Is the outsourcing of data, voice and video communications which include but is not limited to Voice over IP (VoIP or Internet telephony), Instant Messaging (IM), collaboration, video conference applications using fixed and mobile devices, etc.
10. IdaaS – Identity as a Service: Is an authentication infrastructure that is built, hosted and managed by a service provider for the cloud.
11. BaaS – Backup as a Service: Is the backup and recovery services managed by the outside provider.
12. AaaS – Application as a Service: Is an Application Service Provider that provides access to a particular software application over the Internet.
13. EaaS – Everything as a Service: Refers to "X as a service," "anything as a service" or "everything as a service." It is the variety of services and applications emerging for users to access on-demand over the Internet rather than provided locally or on-site. XaaS is the essence of cloud computing.

These models are merely a few of the standard terms used for services within the cloud community.

NIST Service Models

NIST provides a description for three distinct service models. Almost all of the services provided by cloud computing fit into these models:

Software as a Service (SaaS)

SaaS is where the Service Provider provides applications to the client over the Internet. Applications are accessible from various client devices through a thin client interface such as a web browser (e.g., web-based email). In this service model scenario, the consumer does not manage or control the underlying cloud infrastructure including network, servers, operating systems, storage, or critical configuration components. The user can change limited user-specific application configuration settings.

Platform as a Service (PaaS)

PaaS gives the client the ability to deploy onto the cloud infrastructure consumer-created or acquired applications created using programming languages and tools supported by the SP. The user does not manage or control the underlying cloud infrastructure including network, servers, operating systems, or storage, but has control over the deployed applications and possibly application hosting environment configurations.

Infrastructure as a Service (IaaS)

IaaS gives the client the ability to provision processing, storage, networks, and other fundamental computing resources where the consumer can deploy and run arbitrary software, which can include operating systems and applications. The user does not manage or control the underlying cloud infrastructure but has control over operating systems, storage, deployed applications, and possibly limited control of select networking components (e.g., host firewalls).

Deployment Models

Because cloud technology is a consistently evolving paradigm, it is hard to provide an exact definition for the many different variations in cloud deployment models. NIST references four types of deployment models. Most SPs have carved out their niche in the cloud computing business by catering their services around each of the four primary NIST deployment models. The general characteristics of the four types are:

Private Cloud

The private cloud infrastructure is operated solely for an organization. Private clouds can be managed by the community or by a third party. This type of cloud can be administrated on or off the premises.

Community Cloud

A community cloud infrastructure is one that is shared by several organizations. It supports a specific community that has shared concerns. Community clouds can be managed by the community or by a third party. This type of cloud has the option of being administrated on or off the premises.

Public Cloud

The public cloud infrastructure is made available to the public or as a large industry group. Public clouds are owned by organizations who sell cloud services.

Hybrid Cloud

The hybrid cloud infrastructure is a composition of two or more clouds (private, community, or public) that remain unique entities but are bound together by standardized or proprietary technology that enables the best practices from both deployment models. In this model, access can be provided to the community while certain aspects of the cloud can also be held private or public and private clouds can be leveraged to balance the load between clouds.

Some SPs have proprietary hybrid solutions that blend unique deployment models. These solutions are based on a business's organizational structure and location. Some proprietary solutions include storing critical records from the Documentation Control and Retention Department in a local private cloud while general non-critical information is stored in the public cloud. It is important to note that each deployment model should be designed for the type of information that is being handled. Each deployment model has its strengths and weaknesses. For example, a private cloud may not be the most cost-efficient deployment model, but it is preferred because it allows the exertion of additional control over the cloud security and provides distinct levels of privacy. Many regulated organizations in health care such as hospitals, private practices, outpatient services, home health care services or a host of other pharmaceutical companies, chemical companies, medical device companies, hospitals, biotechnology companies, etc. favor the private cloud deployment model because they can readily conform to regulatory standards.

From an organizational standpoint, the number one concern involving computer technology is the protection of regulated data. If your business's data is not in regulatory scope, then your computer systems do not require agency controls. Most companies do not believe that their practices are regulated and therefore do not put regulatory controls in place. However, well over ninety percent of businesses produce information that is governed by a number of different government initiatives. Experienced computer experts implement necessary controls to ensure compliance with government regulations. Mature organizations rely on technical, procedural, organizational, and administrative controls to meet regulatory requirements.

Companies, regulatory agencies, and consumers play a vital role in manufacturing, monitoring, and ensuring products and services are safe. Where the confusion lies is in how safety is perceived and at what point and to what degree security should be implemented to keep information secure. Each entity involved in providing quality products and service may see data protection differently and believe that appropriate resources should be applied to protect their interest.

- From a business perspective, the priority of security surrounding data protection for computer systems would likely be system intellectual property, personal data protection, and national security.
- From the consumer's perspective, the priority of security surrounding data protection for computer systems would be personal protection, system security, and national security.
- From a government perspective, the priority of security surrounding data protection for computer systems is that national security trumps all the other directives. In times of peril and conflict, national security directives are primary directives.

Leveraging the cloud to cut capital expenditure and control operating costs makes it an ideal solution for your business. It is important to understand the various deployment models available on the cloud. There are many different variations in cloud deployment models. The question is which deployment model should be taken into consideration for your design and what are the risks of not conforming to a particular layout. It is important that the deployment model runs parallel with your business objectives.

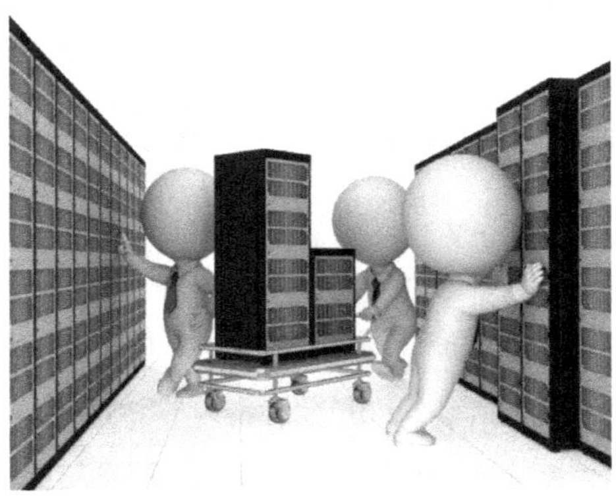

Each deployment model should be designed around the type of information that is being handled. Because cloud technology is consistently evolving, it 's hard to pinpoint all of the variations involved in cloud deployment models. This book cannot explain them all because cloud technology is constantly changing. Some CSPs have proprietary hybrid solutions that blend unique deployment models by providing a solution based on a business's organizational structure and alternative locations. It is important to note that each deployment model should be designed about the type of information that is being handled. Nevertheless, most SPs have carved out their niche in the cloud computing business by focusing their services on one of the four primary NIST service models.

Cloud computing is a means to an end. NIST's description of deployment models, service models, and essential characteristics originated to help develop the first steps in the growth of cloud deployment models. The characterization helps us conceptualize a baseline and serves as a method for comparing cloud services and deployment strategies. Deployment models should complement industry objectives. Deployment, characteristics, and services should be solutions to broader business goals. Access to an extended application, platform, and infrastructure as a service is simply a means to address specific business needs. If a deployment model does not satisfy the requirements for security and privacy, data controls, access, data types, typology, integrity, statutory compliance, trade, and governance, etc., then that business could be throwing resources into the wind. Choosing wrong deployment models can stifle employees, hamper creativity and choke businesses. There is nothing worse than having a cloud solution that is not aligned with business objectives. Business IT solutions are not necessarily situated in one deployment model. Many companies are developing hybrid cloud solutions that contain a plethora of solution-based services.

FDA Information Management (IM) Strategic Plan

The Food and Drug Administration (FDA or Agency) is one of the most information-intensive regulatory agencies in the world. The FDA operates on many continents across the globe. Like most corporations, the FDA is managed through information and distinct processes. Most people think that the FDA's responsibility is limited to ensuring the effectiveness, quality, purity, and safety of food and drug products and services in the US, but do not realize that it operates a complex data information repository in many continents across the globe. Like a living organism, the FDA is constantly growing and ever evolving. It houses one of the largest data knowledge and operations repositories in the world. To have a global presence, it is necessary to establish a hybrid cloud system that complements the agency's activities. Having access to high quality, high availability, high performing data networks, and servers and application infrastructure is an essential requirement for establishing communication services that can be accessed from computer applications, and mobile devices anywhere in the world. Internal workforce capabilities are critical to the FDA's operations, as well as for the integrity of connectivity to the public. Building a private architecture that exhibits real-time connectivity with real-time metrics captured with the major performance indicators (KPIs), dashboards, scorecards, and wireframes is the only way to manage analytics for an ever-expanding repository. It helps in the understanding of each community.

The FDA has decided to reap the benefits of cloud services. It has developed a private cloud solution for managing its disaster recovery activities.13 Currently, the full recovery time for FDA cloud computing resources in the event of a catastrophe is within 45 minutes of discovery. In the case of a virus attack and server failure, data can be restored onto additional configured servers in their environment. The private cloud infrastructure has been developed by the FDA and has been used solely by its organization. No third parties were involved in developing solutions. A senior tech adviser at the FDA said;

> *"An internal cloud approach means that we do not have to pay for costly service contracts with outsourcers, nor do we have to dedicate rooms full of servers to sit idly by just in case of a serious problem."*

Historically, companies that operate in a non-cloud environment would in some cases duplicate dedicated servers as back-ups or use valuable outsourced services. The FDA has decided to develop an internal

[13] (FDA, 2015)

cloud computing disaster recovery approach. This approach allows the agency to backup or restore data in a fraction of the time.

The FDA has many goals for their new data center. One of these goals includes modernizing technology and infrastructure to construct a cloud computing data center that is secure, scalable, elastic, reliable and includes extensive virtualization. An outcome of this initiative has yielded the FDA's first state-of-the-art production data center environment. The new data center gives the FDA the ability to host mission critical servers and computer systems, with fully redundant subsystems (cooling, power, network links, storage, etc.) and compartmentalizes security zones, which are controlled by biometric access control methods. The production data center is inherently less prone to failures due to its fully fault-tolerant cooling, power and network links engineered to exceed 99.995% availability. The FDA proclaims that it will yield less than twenty-seven minutes of downtime per year. The FDA has achieved operational efficiency and cost savings by consolidating servers and virtualizing the environment.

The operational efficiencies include an 89% server reduction through virtualization and a decrease in the number of agency systems. Unlike before, the FDA can run multiple systems on a single high-performance server. The system no longer requires a separate server. Virtualization allows the FDA to reduce the physical server footprint, which demonstrates savings in power consumption costs from a server and data center standpoint. Also, it allows the FDA to utilize equipment and support resources far more efficiently. Some database servers have been consolidated since the onset of cloud service.

There was an 84% reduction of physical equipment. The overall data center infrastructure reliability has increased from 98.3% to 99.9996%, meaning that unscheduled server downtime has been reduced from 6.6 days per calendar year to approximately 30 seconds. The data center consolidations, coupled with forgoing future investments, have saved the FDA $19,706,000.

European Cloud Computing Initiative

The European Union (EU) Commission states that everyone has the right to personal data protection. Whether a person is home watching cable TV, at work on the computer, or at school composing a paper, their electronic fingerprints must be protected. The EU charter states that data protection is a fundamental right, and this right extends to all aspects of life.14

Computer experts must understand that in the EU, everyone has the right to be forgotten. In other words, European data protection rules protect data by enforcing the right to be forgotten. Personal identifying information must not be linked back to a particular person or reside on the network without your permission. Housed data must not be indirectly or directly affiliated with identifying characteristics that are associated with a person. Identifying characteristics include any economic, emotional,

[14] (|, Ferraro, and Carmona, 2015)

behavioral, physical, or social stigmas related to a particular person. It is not merely physical information that's protected, but also any personal data, that indirectly describes a person's conditions or attributes, otherwise known as "a state of being" is protected under EU law.

Data retrieved from various personalized data such as bank accounts, medical records, occupational descriptions, Social Security numbers, photographs, addresses (email or URL), and more that's accessed through various methods, must not linger as fragmented information that's floating around in some computer system. Computer systems, PDAs (Personal Digital Assistants), telephones, emails, websites, IP (internal protocol) addresses, and more are susceptible to penetration or infiltration and must be included in a plan to be deleted.

SPs must design their environment to delete personal data from companies, corporations, and private owners who no longer want data to be processed. Data protection must be seamlessly built into a cloud computing framework. If personal data is not deleted, holders of the data must be explicitly informed about why their data must be kept. Each entity that consumes data must clearly state to the data owner what information is owned. If foreign companies offer goods or services in the EU or monitor the online behavior of citizens, they are responsible for following data protection rules. Data protection rules are not designed to address the individual requirement for handling personal information. EU data protection rules are intended to create a foundation and general approach for providing data handling standards at the national level. Also, companies must actualize a plan for data breaches.

Today's cloud environment is continuously changing. Cloud applications store and share all types of data. Employees and customers are sharing more information than ever before. Employees transport and store personal information on company devices and company information on personal devices. Enforcing data protection in the cloud has become a complex task. It is an ever-evolving security threat that has piqued companies' awareness. Email addresses, phone numbers, employee Social Security numbers, medical histories, credit card numbers, spouse information, billing addresses, birth dates, insurance information, etc., are in the cloud. Small businesses should reassess their security plans to protect themselves against cyber-attacks and malware. The EU has developed data protection rules. They have also enforced a data protection authority to hear cases involving these rules.15 Each EU participating

---

[15] (Metheny, M. (2013) Federal cloud computing)

country has their data protection regulations for processing data protection violations. The EU provides overarching data protection rules with increased responsibility and accountability for those processing confidential, and private data. Confidential or personal information shared with a psychologist, attorney, physician, or therapist must not be divulged to third parties without the express consent of the client. Private data must be free from intrusion into one's personal matters, and personal information privacy is a right rooted in common law.

The European Commission, the executive arm of the EU, believes that cloud computing is the game changer they have been waiting for. The European Commission has determined that cloud computing has the potential to unleash millions of dollars into the economy. The commission has outlined bold initiatives that are expected to deliver millions of European jobs. Cloud computing technology is expected to provide an annual boost to the European economy of approximately €160 billion. The European Commission expects cloud computing to grow the European Gross Domestic Product (GDP) by roughly 1% by 2020.[16]

[16] (COMM, 2016)

The commission's strategy is incredibly ambitious. The approach consists of a multi-prong strategy. The plan is to deploy cloud computing technologies across member nations. The Commission believes that the best way to integrate cloud computing technology into the EU framework is by leveraging the expertise of academia and think tanks combined with the financial wherewithal of the private sector and the implementation of new policies and laws from the government. This entwined relationship is expected to drive creativity, integration, and acceptance of the technology along with establishing a level of trusted certification, interoperability, and collaboration.

The European Commission believes that the stakeholders are best suited to operate and manage cloud technologies. If stakeholders can profit from this new technology, it will grow on its own. In return, the European Commission will not have to pour money into monitoring its growth but will have minimal oversight. The European Commission can focus on ensuring accountability for privacy laws and SLAs. This relationship will give the commission the tools it needs to generate taxable income for managing cloud technologies. Stakeholders, not the EU, will have a vested interest in the availability and the types of technologies being metered in the cloud environment. It is the stakeholders who will determine what services will be successful in the cloud environment because they can determine what services are profitable. The commission's equation has calculated that profitability means success. Governments can tax the success. It is assumed that demand for services such as online music and movie streaming, online banking, education, social networking services, and web-based email will drive profitability.

The European Commission's goal is to utilize key stakeholders and potential investors to unleash the potential of cloud computing in Europe.17 People, businesses, and institutions that want to take the risk can reap the profits from this huge economic windfall. As part of the new strategy to drive European business and government productivity via cloud computing, the European Commission has defined cloud computing as:

> *'Cloud computing' refers to the storage of data (such as text files, pictures and video) and software on remote computers, which users access over the internet on the device of their choice. This is faster, cheaper, more flexible and potentially more secure than on-site IT solutions.*[18]

The European Commission understands the potential impact that cloud computing can have on their economy and the benefits of making computer technology secure, scalable, elastic, reliable, available, faster, and cheaper. Cloud computing has the potential to change the way Europeans operate their business and conduct services within their businesses. Companies can determine the way in which their services are being delivered. Stakeholders can offer a unique mix of product and services and, thus, win big. The commission is encouraging interested parties and investors to step up to the plate, make the initial investment and take ownership of this economic windfall. The European Commission plans to support stakeholders by working through a myriad of regulations and establishing laws and policies that enhance growth and achieve

[17] (COMM, 2016b)

[18] (COMM, 2012)

meaningful infrastructure changes that facilitate a host of cloud-based products and services.

Trying to create a path towards EU acceptance of cloud computing, for all of its members, can be extremely challenging. The European Commission is taking measures to understand better the technical and social challenges that may be inhibiting companies from entering into this new phenomenon. There are a lot of unrealized legal challenges surrounding cloud computing in the European region. The European Commission is committed to removing any regional challenges inhibiting the growth of cloud computing and to strengthening regulations surrounding data compliance, data protection and portability, copyright laws, geographical restrictions, etc. The cloud architecture must be designed such that European privacy laws are not violated. Procedural controls, technical controls, administrative controls, and organizational structure all play a role in ensuring the transparency, confidentiality integrity, and availability of personal information.

However, not everyone believes that the new privacy laws will achieve cloud growth. Many entities feel that EU laws governing data privacy and restrictions on cloud integration are far more restrictive than those in the US. It is believed that the EU initiative governing privacy challenges the open cloud concept. It restricts hybrid solutions that circumvent the legal framework by creating illusive data paths. Nevertheless, when designing an appropriate deployment model, EU laws governing data privacy and developing a cloud typology must be considered.

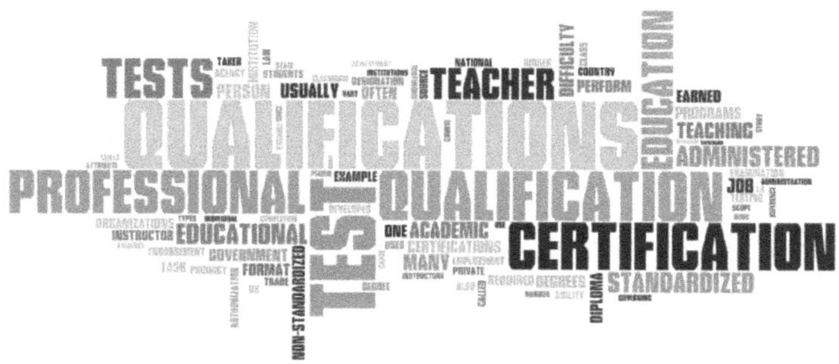

The magnitude of services being offered in the cloud is unimaginable. Communities are mesmerized by it, and it continues to challenge our curiosity. The cloud phenomenon is not limited to individuals or any one European region, but it has the profound effect on the way we do business and how we live. Cloud computing is integrated into the fabric of Europeans' lives. It has an unseen grasp on all aspects of European existence. Businesses use it to make their processes more efficient. Consumers want to try and enjoy different technologies. Governments want to simplify cloud infrastructure by deconstructing delivery of services for ease of taxing cloud technologies at specific operational nodes. The challenge for the EU is ensuring that privacy laws are not violated as data flows from one jurisdiction to another. Who has control over that data? Where is the data processed, stored, and what security and privacy arrangements have been made? What technical, regulatory, privacy and security requirements must be met? Should the location where the data originated be held responsible for meeting all of the requirements, or should the EU establish a set of overarching laws and data standards?

EU Technical Standards

Technical standards inhibit the acceptance of cloud computing technology in Europe. Having different technical standards for each European region will affect how IT environments interoperate. Suppose you decide to move an application between clouds. Some challenges might be that the target cloud:

1. Must be able to support the application
2. Must not change the application's functionality
3. Must retain the same security controls
4. Must be able to rebuild the application stack
5. Must be able to manipulate encrypted data

The software application must be able to interoperate between clouds. Interoperation is essential for the acceptance of the cloud computing technology. Without collaboration among member states to encourage interoperability among cloud networks, cloud development would virtually come to a complete stop. The flow of investments into cloud technology would trickle.

The EU officially recognizes the European Telecommunications Standards Institute (ETSI) as a major player in shaping technical standards.19 ETSI produces globally-applicable standards for Information and Communications Technologies (ICT), including fixed, mobile, radio, converged, broadcast and Internet technologies. ETSI also provides quality of service metrics and monitoring capabilities that aid in determining the effectiveness of cloud communication services. Quality services, such as

---

[19] *(Schlosser et al., 2009)*

speed, accuracy, availability, reliability, security, simplicity, flexibility, capability, usability, fidelity, etc., are a crucial part of the cloud experience lifecycle. The European Commission has made it a priority to streamline and reduce the red tape behind the acceptance of standards that govern the quality of service of Europeans' cloud computing experience. Developing a set of quality of service metrics that can be used as the gold standard for measuring cloud capabilities would help standardize performance expectations for all European nations.

In the cloud, deployment models, characteristics, and cloud services consist of a host of interoperating elements. These features range from small devices up to supercomputers. The elements serve individuals, multinational corporations, and global communities.

Each entity participates in the service of data, information, and knowledge to and from every country in the world. To reduce the red tape behind the regional member states' acceptance of cloud standards, the European Commission aims to conduct front-end research to identify technical complexities and legal conflict among countries. It is their belief that by identifying and reducing the complexities behind technical standards, greater interoperability, data portability, and security will be achieved.

The acceptance of technical standards allows users across the EU to normalize their communication backbone. It sets a level of expectation for everyone within the European cloud community. Establishing requirements for speed, accuracy, availability, reliability, security, simplicity, flexibility, capability, usability, fidelity, etc. gives investors and developers the confidence that certain products and services will perform as expected. Developers can align their products and services around network capabilities. There is no benefit in providing online gaming to a community whose network is incapable of processing it.

Certification Programs

The European Commission is also encouraging certification. Certification must be established for the stakeholders to discern the trustworthiness of the cloud environment. Data is transported across huge distances, from one cloud provider to another, utilizing various technologies. It is imperative that integrity is verified through certification. The European Commission believes that development and recognition for

EU-wide certification programs for the trustworthiness of cloud providers are essential for growing their industry.

The EU continues to promote a legal structure that requires certification of cloud service providers. The EU is working towards providing a legal framework that would require certification of cloud service providers. Eventually, it will be a prerequisite for SPs to substantiate specific industry standards and safeguards to ensure the quality of data. Certification and SLAs measure the trustworthiness of the process and ensure that cloud service providers are complying with their obligations.

Creating an environment for investigating technical standards, SLAs, and certifications lay the groundwork that will establish a compliant cloud computing environment. By planting the seeds for the start-up compliance, the hope is that this effort will empower regulatory authorities to create certifying bodies. These administrators can identify and flush out SPs that are not living up to the requirements contained in theSLA, and that are not providing an expected quality of service. Trust is at the heart of the cloud experience. The European Commission believes that the SP will certify that they are abiding by the standards that are required. Certifications are at the core of that faith. SPs must comply with legal obligations and must be certified.

The European Commission believes that transparency with stakeholders will aid in the promotion of trusted cloud sources. Certification will also allow the mapping of similar technical specifications and create a framework across the global environment. Thus, increasing the interoperability of cloud technologies will automatically mature scalability requirements. Certification will allow regulating bodies to adopt standards for which to guide and promote cloud activities and create a baseline of performance metrics on which cloud service providers can operate. Europeans are expected to rely on certifying bodies to determine the trustworthiness of the cloud service provider. In addition to SLAs and certification, CSPs must comply with legal audit requirements for applications and systems. CSPs must submit to governance and oversight to ensure reliability and trustworthiness.

Service level agreements

The European Commission's model for cloud computing revolves around the SLA between the SP and the European Commission.20 Development of quality expectations and fair contract terms are the basis for establishing hosting arrangements between the contract service provider and the European Commission. During the certification period, the contract service provider must provide the European Commission with evidence from a test that has evaluated the quality of service. With the explosion of the cloud environment and the plethora of new technologies,

---

[20] *(YOUR RIGHTS AS A DATA SUBJECT WHAT CAN YOU DO IF YOUR RIGHTS ARE VIOLATED DATA TRANSFERS TO NON-EU COUNTRIES USEFUL ADDRESSES AND NUMBERS*

there is no better way to control the interaction and collaboration among SPs than with theSLA.

The SLA is a legally binding negotiated document that sets real expectations for services that are offered to the customer. Expectations for speed, accuracy, availability, reliability, security, simplicity, flexibility, capability, usability, and fidelity should be discussed in the contract. The best cloud services are the ones that have their obligations verified in writing and are capable of being measured. Because the environment is in continuous flux, the SLA is the only way of determining a Quality of Service along with guaranteeing privacy and protection. The European Commission is the progenitor of cloud products and services across the EU. However, they also view themselves as the end client of the offered service. The SLA is in place for the duration of the contract and should include but not be limited to specifics surrounding:

1. Response Time: A mechanism should be put in place to determine how many users can concurrently use the service for a given period.
2. Programmed and Unexpected Downtime: Notifications for downtime and interruptions (such as sabotage, natural disasters, and unforeseen events) as well as maintenance should be communicated to the European Commission over a defined period.
3. Availability of Services: Content Service Providers must determine the length of time in which applications are available to users. The availability, rate and cost of the measurement period must be part of the metrics.
4. Monthly Hosting Reports: A monthly report covered in the above descriptions is to be submitted to the commission.

The European Commission would like the SLA to serve as a starting point for defining engineering and operational commitments. The service level specifications implemented by the Commission examine mechanisms placed by service level management, service level enforcement, as well as standard language and modeling.

The European Commission considers the SLAs to be a tool for gauging the quality and the type of service. This reasoning accrues because of the agreement between the SP and the European Commission. The SLA is a contract that provides an agreement for services that are approved by both parties. The agreement is predicated on establishing ongoing internal metrics that determine the quality of service.

The EU can provide metrics to organizations so that they can differentiate mediocre SPs from those that have a competitive edge. Developing an SLA lifecycle will help the commission to gauge cloud capabilities better while developing a policy that will better implement cloud computing technology. Cloud systems provide a plethora of new technologies and services. Most services being offered in the cloud have never used this mode of delivery. Standard expectations will aid in developing new technologies that are offered on-demand. With providers, brokers, customers, etc., the best way to monitor expectations, objectives, challenges, and usage patterns within the ecosystem is to implement SLAs. The Commission believes that SLAs are the way to establish:

1. Goals through Quality of Service (QoS).
2. Privacy and protection constraints through Quality of Protection (QoP). [21]

3. Expectations through the description of actions. According to the QoS, this is a necessity to deliver the service.
4. Responsibilities through the inclusion of obligations of parties including penalties and exclusion terms.
5. Evolvement cases through the definition of rules that enable efficient adaptation of resource provisioning based on the changing demands of the applications and the end users.

Partnership

The European Commission is not in the business of purchasing and managing a publicly run data center. Nor does it propel a particular architecture for deployment models, service models, or force design characteristics down the throats of European consumers. Cloud stakeholders fundamentally determine how IT is delivered and consumed. The purpose of the partnership is to combine resources, expertise suppliers, and vendors so that the conversation begins.

> *"Cloud computing is a game-changer for our economy. Without EU action, we will stay stuck in national fortresses and miss out on billions in economic gains. We must achieve critical mass and a single set of rules across Europe. We must tackle the perceived risks of cloud computing head-on."* [22]

The European Commission is inviting public authorities and industry leaders, cloud buyers, and technology suppliers into a European cloud partnership. As stated before, this partnership is responsible for establishing cloud standards. These standards include, but are not limited to, security, interoperability, and procurement. The Commission would like

[21] (|, Ferraro, and Carmona, 2015)
[22] (COMM, 2017)

these partners to provide criteria for performance, design, functional specifications, and architecture of the cloud.

> *"Europe needs to think big. The cloud strategy will enhance trust in innovative computing solutions and boost a competitive digital single market where Europeans feel safe. That means a swift adoption of the new data protection framework which the Commission proposed earlier this year and the development of safe and fair contract terms and conditions."*[23]

Cloud computing is an ever evolving long-term paradigm. Most people do not understand the capabilities nor its limitations. Its existence has forged the emergence of new technologies and services. This cyber technology supplants a previous generation of old centralized IT processing models. Cloud computing has helped us move away from a centralized computing model, where the user is the manager, to a place where everything is managed by someone else. The European Commission does not want to impose their vision of cloud computing technology but would like to spur communication between the public and the private sector. This communication will hopefully create an environment where technology providers will engage with business partners, vendors, users, customers, and CSPs in ways never seen before. Cloud computing can soar. The growth and profitability of cloud computing are best monitored through SLAs. SLAs govern how CSPs interact with the public and private sector and regulate provisioning, collaboration, and interaction by defining the terms of engagement for participating entities. It is easy to define deployment

---

[23] (European, no date)

models, characteristics, and services the cloud provides, but there is more than meets the eye than what is in the definition.

Chapter 2

Best Practices

At last he had found the Regulatory Guidelines.

Cloud computing platforms are attractive because they let users quickly access hosted private and public resources on demand without the complexities and time associated with the purchase, installation, configuration and deployment of traditional physical infrastructure. Cloud architects dream of building the ultimate high-tech cloud-networking environment. Given free reign, architects would incorporate all types of bells and whistles to make cloud computing an awesome experience. This begs us to ask the question, what essential requirements does Cloud

Computing need to have to make it an excellent experience.[24] What we are asking is, what are the necessary requirements needed to ensure acceptability of cloud networks? What are the minimum requirements needed to drive the functionality and acceptance of cloud network among User communities? Every computerized system has its unique set of requirements (technical, security, architectural, business, regulatory, functional, configuration, data, user, and more).

"The hospital computer system has a virus. Ironic, isn't it?"

If you could design a cloud system and incorporate state-of-the-art bells and whistles into its functionality, what would your Cloud look like? Would you build a semi-open design that would allow users to move in and out of the cloud to access software services on demand or a very rigid design where security is a priority and everything is accessed by multiple

[24] Sekaran, C.K. (2014)

passwords? Would you leverage hardware as a service by utilizing the external SPs storage capacity, IT services, compute power, private infrastructure, firewall, virus protection, on-demand services, etc. or would you make these resources available onsite at your current location, under your control? What design criteria, technical standards, and best practices would you like to see used as a blueprint for your Cloud environment.

Best practices are simply a set of industry-accepted tools that are used to promulgate Cloud activities. Best practices help govern the functionality and performance of the Cloud network. Best practices are industry-accepted standards that define how data, security, support, and other system services are rendered. They drive the enjoyment of the computer experience. Most users do not realize they exist. Areas in which Best practices are exhibited include but are not limited to:

1. Security: Security is the foundation for building trust in the Cloud. Users want to know that their personal information is secure. For the most part, security logs are integrated in every aspect of the system's operation that contains enough information to verify Internal and external activities.
2. System support: User would like to have their existing platform seamlessly integrate into traditional IT systems. Through virtualization, system support personnel are available to ensure that access to hardware, virtualization, and software solutions found at the data centers can flow to the user's desktop in a seamless fashion so, that they can deliver products and services.
3. Procedures and policies: Everyone wants knowledgeable employees. Operational procedures ensure that employees are trained and empowered to initiate, escalate and resolve conflicts. Procedures, policies, guidelines, etc., help employees to provide technical, administrative and customer based solutions.

4. SLA: The SLA governs the SPs business relationship. The SLA is built upon sound metrics that can be easily measured and consistently met. These parameters are visible and accessible to all stakeholders.
5. Metering services: Having metering rules that quantify services and offerings reduce customer service problems help with billing offerings and quality of service issues.
6. Complexity: Cloud services must not be sophisticated. Service boundaries/portals should be seamless to the user and administrators and easy to navigate. No one likes to remember endless passwords and usernames, security keys, encryption notices, etc.
7. Monitoring: Observing the health of the system helps determine bottlenecks and peak usage. People should be able to assess the health of their environment at any time.
8. Expansion: Using internal metrics to determine what type of growth you should be expecting in the coming years. No one wants to be put in the position of not being able to increase the load.
9. Dynamically serviced: Strive for a virtual environment that is dynamically maintained. An environment that provides maximum efficiency and performance without manual intervention will reduce headaches.
10. Accessibility: Users expect the Cloud network to be accessible, reliable and available twenty-four hours a day.
11. Management tools: Tools used for provisioning back end operations such as billing and system management must be interfaced correctly. No one wants to call back and talk to five people to resolve account problems.
12. Redundancy: Redundant solutions must be seen as failsafe measures.
13. Change management: Make sure that no changes are made with how your knowledge. All administrative actions should be recreated using the activities data trail.

14. Organization: Your organization must be adequately resourced. Assess your organization's ability to accommodate daily throughput and extreme demands.
15. Facilities utilities and equipment (FU&E): Assess your facilities utilities and equipment to ensure they are operating as expected and that environmental conditions are optimal.

If designers, developers, architects, integrators, manufacturers, etc., utilize the above best practices, everyone would be in complete alignment and computer systems could interoperate seamlessly. If the security complexities of your PC are similar to my computer system, then we both could send the same e-mail s to each other without it being mistaken for spam. Encrypted data packets can be encoded and decoded into bits and routed between systems using an established connection for similar applications. Companies look to best practices to improve their competitiveness. Integrators want solutions that can be easily incorporated into the existing IT environment and with other applications and solutions that promote maximum interoperability. Companies want to implement best practices that will allow for easy implementation with quick time to market and return on investment. Best practices help to create an environment in which there is rapid application development, which supports rapid design, build, test, and deployment methodologies.

The problem with the above fast-paced environment is that they only address computer implementation goals that are based only on business and user needs. The technology behind computer system design and cloud architecture is driven by the need to exchange information across nations, governments, industries, businesses, and families. Everyone wants to build a bigger, better, and faster network that is secure, scalable, functional, expandable, and interoperable.

Problems with the Cloud

The problem with committing to the concept that bigger is better is that it does not adequately address regulatory requirements. Regulatory requirements surrounding data privacy and the right to forget are being pushed into the background[25]. These requirements are not included in the system's planning phase. Regulatory requirements are taking a second seat to business and user needs. In most cases, regulatory professionals are not present during the system's planning and design phases. As computer systems become more centralized, regulations governing data privacy and

[25] (Jones, 2016)

confidentiality become nonexistent in the computer system's operational framework.

Data is collected across multiple regions at an extremely fast pace and in large quantities. Each geographical area that data passes through has different laws for handling information. Sifting through bits of information and metadata to help determine if the information is original, what is its point of origin, who created it, who has access to it, and where the information resides is a challenging task, especially if we are talking about a hybrid Cloud solution where confidential private and public information is indiscriminately shared. Under these conditions, it can be an extremely daunting task for a company to enforce data privacy and the right-to-forget laws into a third-party integrated Cloud system. The irony is that, even though individual bits are untraceable, they can be combined to form an abstract profile. I do not have to know where your personal information came from to access your personal records. Complex data searches can get together bits and pieces of your profile in a matter of days. Those bits and pieces of information can be used to make predictions about your behavior in the future.

The excitement surrounding uploading information into the Cloud slowly dissipates when bits and pieces of private and confidential information cannot be fully retracted or when bits of information can be pieced together to develop an electronic profile of your personal self and business activities. Bits and pieces of public and private information in the Cloud can have huge legal ramifications. Once information is placed in cyberspace, it can rarely be fully retracted. A set of best practices for regulated industries that govern the use of personal and private information does exist. Each governing region has regulatory controls in place that govern how information must be handled. Regulatory oversight controls are not just limited to the design, build, test and deployment methodologies of networked systems only, but they also include instructions and controls over how data is being managed by these systems.

Regulatory authorities are not in the business of driving ingenuity and creativity for Cloud design. No regulatory agency will propose an architecture or design requirements because technology innovation it is not within their core competency. They specialize in regulating and taxing and not creating technologies. However, agencies have developed a set of requirements and expectations for companies who operate computer systems in regulated spaces. Governments, supporting agencies and private standards groups develop universal controls or specifications for businesses whose systems manage controlled information. If you are designing a computerized system from scratch or purchasing a new out-of-the-box computer system for a regulated space, regulatory agencies want to know your development methodology, process supporting the system, security controls, maintenance, governance and record management process. Players in the regulated space including but not limited to companies such as biological, medical devices, cosmetics, pharmaceuticals, diagnostics, healthcare, food and beverage, clinical trials, life sciences, nutraceuticals, nuclear, etc., have their independent legal framework containing specific data management requirements. If you desire to do business in the regulatory space, it is important that you first understand data requirements for your products and services.

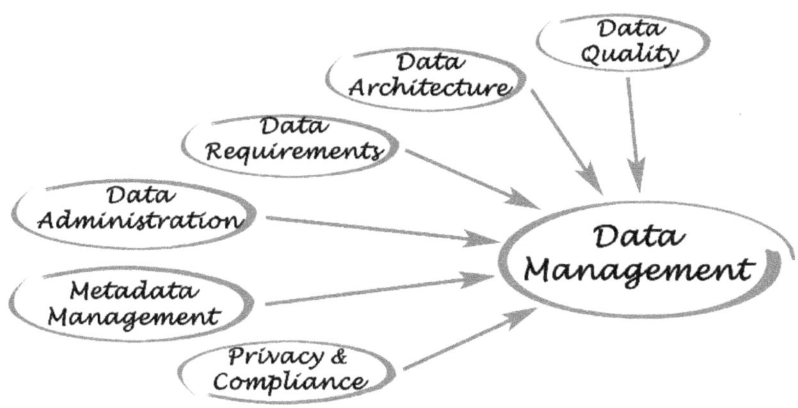

Data Quality

Regulatory agencies spend hundreds of millions of dollars scrutinizing the conditions under which regulated information is being generated, accessed, controlled, stored, retrieved, etc. These agencies want to make sure that the conditions under which information is processed ensure data confidentiality, privacy, security, integrity, authenticity, reliability, legibility, and data availability[26]. If regulated information resides on your computer system, then it's crucial that you take to heart the information below. If your Cloud or computer system can ensure that the design meets the following data requirements, then you're several steps ahead of the crowd

1. Data Privacy: Data Privacy is also called Information Privacy. Regulatory authorities want to make sure except where required by regulation, court order, or applicable law, an entity must not rent, sell, or share your personal information and will make every reasonable attempt to safeguard your privacy.
2. Data Security; Regulatory authorities want to ensure that adequate physical and technological safeguards are in place to prevent data being used for purposes for which the owner has not given consent and to protect data from destructive forces. This includes tracing unwanted actions of users.
3. Data Integrity: Data integrity must consist of maintaining and assuring the accuracy and completeness of data. You should adopt some form of redundancy to verify the integrity of data.
4. Data Authenticity: Cloud data originates from multiple sources. Nevertheless, there must be some level of assurance that data has not been corrupted after its creation. The raw or readable data is what it claims to be.
5. Data Confidentiality: Regulators want some level of assurance that data that is not made available or disclosed to unauthorized

---

1. [26] (Olson and White, 2002)

individuals, entities, or processes. In extreme cases, data needs to be scrubbed from personal identifiers not to divulge participants.

6. Data Reliability: Is the process of ensuring that data is sufficiently complete and error free. It attests to the trustworthiness of a record as a statement of fact.
7. Data Availability: Copies or original Records must be made available to regulatory agencies available for inspection and copying any reasonably within a reasonable period.
8. Data legibility: A quality of the data that ensures that its content can be interpreted correctly due to the known and distinct attributes.

Regulatrs spend an excruciating amount of time reviewing submitted data. The regulatory process centers around the legitimacy of the information presented to the agency. There is no sticker on the side of a computer system guaranteeing that information in your computer system has been qualified to meet government requirements for data confidentiality, data privacy, security, integrity, authenticity, reliability, legibility, and availability. No manufacturer post data requirements on a label affixed to the computer saying, "This system has been qualified to ensure that your data meets all regulatory requirements. You cannot buy a system that is preconfigured to guarantee data privacy out of the box. Regulatory requirements are incorporated into the systems functionality based upon how it is being integrated into the environment.

Encryption may be embedded into the functionality of one component in your system. Nevertheless, it is false to assume that because individual components or one computer has some form of built-in security and is compatible with other systems that whole system must be compliant. Most people feel that all they need to do is assemble the parts, and presto, the computer system is ready to process personal and private information.

"Davy, we need someone to fight off industry regulations."

Security vs. Privacy

One of the weaknesses of the cloud is that security does not guarantee privacy. The problem with implementing identity and access management, data-loss prevention, real-time web security, e-mail security, intrusion management, security assessments, security information and event management, encryption, business continuity, disaster recovery, and network security is that they are excellent security measures but none of them can address the right to forget.

Just because the your network is secure from an accessibility or role perspective, does not mean that the flow of personal and private information is controlled and traceable to the right parties and across the right regions. Most Cloud computer security is based upon a business hierarchy. The higher in the organization you are, the more access you have. Others are hybrid systems where there is some form of hierarchical access. However, most employees are subject to access that is based on roles and privileges, where your role in the company allows you to access certain privileges that are associated with your job function. An overwhelming majority of computer security access initiatives cater to role-based access. [27]

These systems are concerned with protecting access not necessarily privacy. There is a hidden assumption that if you limit access then you will provide privacy. That is not necessarily true in the Cloud. Clouds can contain bits and pieces of anything about everything. When you pool these bit and pieces together you can build a profile from which you can make a fairly accurate assessment.

There are various laws in place that specifically govern how regulated data must be processed. Regional and international restrictions that govern data identification, traceability, and flow of information must be pushed further into the Cloud design framework and included in the systems workflow. Most architects assumed that role based accessibility requirements should be enough. The assumption is that if a user can be identified, and their actions can be tracked in an audit trail, then the

---

[27] (Stalla-Bourdillon, Phillips, and Ryan, 2014b)

network data is traceable and regulatory requirements are met. Today's regulatory framework is a little more complex. It requires that cloud typologies take into considerations regional and international nuances that govern the processing and sharing of information. Computer systems and applications must rely on meta-data and datasets for traceability. Being ill informed of the regulations can create a false sense of security.

"Frankly, you are so far sighted that you can see the future of healthcare."

Most people get it! The Cloud must be secure. No one should be able to access personal or private data without proper authorization. Personal and private data are located in a secure location that is only accessible by senior administrators. The administrators have privileges to backup and archive information into a secure area. Here are just a few questions you might want to ask.

1. Have you downloaded and stored someone's personal information on your computer system?

2. Have you accessed and downloaded confidential, private, secure, classified, or internal information onto your computer system
3. Have you downloaded copies of music media (MP3) files, film and video files, etc, without appropriate approval?
4. Does the migration of data to this location violate regional and international data requirements or infringe any copyright, database rights, trademarks or other intellectual property?
5. Is your Quality department included in approving an agreement with a service provider?
6. Has an assessment been completed to determine if the flow of data to and from your location violate regional or international data requirements?
7. Is the storage location accessible to regulatory authorities for inspection and document review within a reasonable period?
8. Are there any special requirements that dictate copies or original data be located onsite or offsite?
9. Is a yearly audit conducted to assess the compliance to the SLA and internal compliance?
10. Does the migration of data to this location violate regional and international data requirements?
11. Is the storage location accessible to regulatory authorities within a reasonable period?
12. Are there requirements that dictate which copies of data need to be located onsite?
13. Does this violate any SLAs?
14. Are pedigrees being provided for access to the information?
15. Are the retention periods satisfied at the service provider's location?
16. is the system equipped to invoke " right to forget." in line with the informed consent?
17. Where is the original data processed and stored; this includes metrics, statistical analysis, and analytics?

18. Where did the data originate?
19. Are there different laws, compliance and processing requirements levied on your electronic information?
20. Is additional meta-data attached to your information that identifies its point of origin or the reconstruction of its path?
21. Will informed consent follow personal information?
22. Does your data receive the same handling instructions and applied the same way in every region it crosses?
23. When your electronic information is processed, is it stored or buffered without your consent?
24. Are there any restrictions or filtering applied when processing your electronic information that could lead to data integrity questions?
25. If data is being cleaned what are the cleaning standards?
26. Are additional non-validated processes that your electronic information is subject to result in inaccuracies?
27. Is archived information being replicated or destroyed?
28. Does the Audit Trail track meta-data and fragments of information?

Make sure you have a complete understanding of your regulatory framework. Regulations help to promulgate Cloud-computing acceptance more than anything else does. Sure, the Cloud is a very good idea but, having a technically secure data transaction with no regulatory and policy restrictions on how the information will be used can cause some serious legal issues downstream. If computing cannot be designed to meet regulatory requirements, then it would cease to be seen as a safe vehicle to exchange information. In the regulatory space, the need for data confidentiality, data privacy, data security, data integrity, data authenticity, data reliability, legibility, and data availability is just as important as the need to build a bigger, better and faster network that is secure, scalable, functional, expandable, and interoperable. A computing system that is secure but not compliant is superfluous.[28]

Regulatory Goals

There are over two-hundred regulatory authorities in the world. When doing business in highly regulated industries, there is one thing that you stumble upon very quickly, the laws, rules, guidance, policies and standards created by regulatory agencies are not just applicable to one particular business sector.

Data Integrity is currently the number one major global concern of Health Authorities and the pharmaceutical industry. Data integrity coumponded with the Lack of awareness of regulatory requirements, employee errors, failure to check accuracy of data, software or system

---

[28] (Snedaker and Rogers, 2006)

malfunction, configuration problems with electronic data handling or malfeasance by employees can lead to data integrity issues

Some Regulations have broad applications across many different industries. For the most part, statutory interpretations can contain global assumptions about how things are supposed to work. In most cases, these global assumptions have related applications across many industry sectors. For example, the FDA's interpretation or computer security (21 CFR Part 11 Guidance on Electronic Records and Signatures)[29] has applicability in the healthcare arena but, it does not contradict the government's requirements for computer security for nuclear, banking, and other industry sectors. For the most part, each regulatory framework complements each other. All regulated environments require that information systems have procedural, administrative, organizational, and technical controls in place for maintaining control over business processes.

The FDA's requirement for security surrounding computer systems used in the food industry is similar to that employed in the drug industry. Likewise, a computer system located in the Department of Defense (DOD) has some of the same fundamental security characteristics as a system similar to the systems at the FDA. Both systems require passwords, virus protection, backups, archiving, contingency planning, audits, and more. The DOD may have a more elaborate and sophisticated security scheme in place but, for the most part, both agencies fundamental security policies are essentially similar.

---

[29] (McDowall, 2002)

Unlike the the regulations in the financial industry, the Food and Drug Agency does not consider computer system security its primary directive. Financial institutions must go to great lengths to protect financial information. Federal Reserve Banks are fiscal agents of the United States. They are authorized by the Department of the Treasury to perform the necessary activities to carry out US objectives. Financial institutions are ever monitoring the effectiveness of their computer system architecture and security, in the light of banking requirements. There is no question that financial disclosure and Sarbanes-Oxley Act (SOX)[30] - corporate accountability are important concerns to the FDA, but we must undeerstand why security is nt the agencies top concern. While computer security is a primary concern, the FDA considers patient safety their number one mission directive. Patient safety, coupled with data integrity and privacy, is the driver behind all FDA legislation. Regulations in the healthcare industry are very detailed and if broken are punishable by law. Regulations governing the transport of drug products kick in the minute you start transporting drug products across the state line. The reason why food, drug, cosmetic, and medical device legislation is so anal is that there have been some deaths in the healthcare industry resulting from drug mix-ups.

---

[30] (Green and Millstein, 2004)

The FDA believes that if they can introduce uniform legislation, policies and guidance that clearly spell out how businesses are expected to conduct drug discovery, development, clinical testing, manufacturing, and marketing then the consumer is more likely to receive safe and effective products. If consumers are happy, then drug manufacturers can focus on finding ways to make drug products safer and more available. Building a computing system that is aligned with the FDA's regulatory expectations make good business sense. Computer systems must be designed with the FDA's primary directive in mind—patient safety. If your Cloud System has been tested (validated or qualified) and procedures are written to provide with a high degree of assurance that it provides confidentiality, privacy, security, integrity, authenticity, reliability, legibility, and data availability to protect regulated information, then it is apt to pass regulatory scrutiny. Computer systems must be tested to ensure that system data is trustworthy, and its functionality is aligned with its intended use. Procedures that define how businesses execute backups, restores, audit trails, archiving, electronic records and signatures, must be designed and tested. Cloud network design must be tested to ensure the functionality is aligned with regulatory objectives.

The FDA sees computer security and financial accountability as a means of achieving patient safety. As discussed above, the theme driving the development of FDA regulatory policy is centered on patient safety. Just like the United States, the Commission, and EU countries consider patient safety a priority. They have put initiatives in place to better understanding patient needs. However, the crux or the theme driving cloud computing legislation in the European arena is centered on data privacy and data protection. The Commission and EU countries and the United States are beating a similar drum. European computer networks must consider the EC law and EU regional regulatory requirements. In Europe, the primary theme driving regulations in the communications, IT, and healthcare industry is centered on data privacy and data protection.

Therefore, if we understand the underlying theme driving EU and U.S. legislation (data privacy, data protection, and patient safety), we can design a Cloud computer system that will pass regulatory agencies audits and inspections. As long as we do not forget the prime directives, we can pretty much guarantee that all remaining guidance, policies, and additional legislation will support the prime directives.

The remainder of this chapter will focus on providing an overview of the primary regulations driving the use and integration of computing technologies for biotech, chemical companies, pharmaceuticals, drug device companies, nuclear industries, and health care. It will also provide a basic understanding about how regulatory authorities scrutinize computer systems and discuss some minimum requirements for information systems that are in regulated spaces. Biological, medical devices, cosmetics, pharmaceuticals, diagnostics, healthcare, food & beverage, clinical trials, life sciences, and nuclear companies have independent legal frameworks containing unique nuances. The information provided in this chapter focuses on the spirit of industry standards and intent of the law. Even though regulations, policies, guidance, and interpretations may echo similar intentions, it is important to understand that there are small distinctions surrounding each complementary framework. This chapter contains case studies that are unique to the healthcare industry but applicable in the other industries

Chapter 3

Healthcare

"Have you hammered out the new rule book yet?"

Electronic Records/Electronic Signatures (21 CFR Part 11)[31], FDA Guide on General principle of validation[32], (CFR) Part 820, Quality System regulation QSR[33], and the FDA Guide on Computerized Systems Used in Clinical Trials etc, are just some of the many federal codes and guidance documents created by the FDA to explain the agency's position on computer systems for regulated industries. These documents contain legal precedence and direction on what security measures and processes must

---

[31] (Santoro, Robin, and Administration, 2002)
[32] (Guidance for industry process validation: General principles and practices, 2011)
[33] (Center and Health, 2016)

be established for entities who want to do business in the regulated space. Regulatory agencies realize that the tools (software, hardware, instruments, devices, computer systems, etc.) used to measure scientific phenomena needs to be tested to ensure they are working properly. If we are using software to determine how many white blood cells are on the tip of a needle and are processing or sending that data to the Cloud, then that computer system must be inspected to ensure its working as expected. Because Cloud computer systems are used to process and manage regulatory records developers, architects, administrators, users, or anybody who has access to those records must adhere to regulatory requirements.

The FDA food and drug administration issue hundreds of guidance documents every year. Each paper explains the agency's interpretation or policy on a particular subject. This chapter is not geared to create experts in the area of FDA law nor on the regulations governing the pharmaceutical, healthcare, biopharmaceutical, medical device, hospitals and biotechnology industries. The purpose of this chapter is to expose you to the underlying policies, guidance, interpretations, and laws that drive the acceptance of computer systems in regulated spaces. Just because a company can integrate a Cloud Computing network into an environment does not mean that the system is aligned with regulatory agencies expectations. This chapter helps to shape the understanding that cloud computing technology, must comply with requirements from the regulatory agencies that have jurisdiction over your activities before it is considered acceptable.

In the United States, the confidentiality, privacy, security, integrity, authenticity, reliability, legibility, and data availability of any record, is necessary, especially if the records prove that processes and products are safe and effective. In the European Community, data privacy and data security support confidential and personal information are major factors that must be given high consideration. Pay close attention to the regulations, policies codes, rules, and standards in this chapter. Failure to comply with regulatory requirements can lead to imprisonment. The questions that are being discussed in the following section are:

1. What are some of the regulations that should drive the design of computer systems?
2. To what degree should we test the functionality, operational effectiveness, and performance of computer systems?
3. Does how the system is being used have an effect on its installation?
4. Beyond installation what should the businesses do to ensure the trustworthiness of records?

The pharmaceutical and nuclear industries are the most heavily regulated industries in the world. These industries report to many regulating bodies. Health care providers have one of the strictest and most heavily regulated businesses spaces. Large volumes of legislation are targeted at specific practices in the healthcare industry. Regulatory agencies provide procedures, best practices, standards, guidance, policies, etc. to ensure consumers are exposed to products and processes that are safe, pure, and effective. Adhering to good practices makes good sense because medication errors in the healthcare industry are common. Extending back in history, the healthcare industry has been plagued with unsafe practices such improper prescribing, ineffective processes and procedures, inaccurate prescriptions, faulty distribution, inadequate packaging, incorrect labeling, invalid compounding, erroneous distribution, negligent monitoring, use, etc. These mishaps have led to disastrous outcomes. Many think that scrutiny and strict oversight of the healthcare activities are long overdue being justified by some facts below:

1. Mostly children died taking an Elixir Sulfanilamide containing the poisonous liquid, diethylene glycol. Elixer Sulfanilamide, contains a toxic liquid, diethylene, causing the deaths of 107 people. [34]
2. Nearly 300 deaths and injuries resulted from the use of sulfathiazole tablets, an antibiotic, tainted with phenobarbital.
3. A nationwide investigation by the FDA revealed that chloramphenicol, an antibiotic, caused nearly 180 cases of deadly blood diseases.
4. Thalidomide, in sleeping pill, caused severe birth defects of affecting the arms and legs in thousands of babies.
5. Up until 1993 drug, companies were not required to include women of childbearing potential in research toward determining gender-specific effects. Drugs were administered without compensation for the patient's age or sex.
6. Up until 1998, pharmaceutical companies were not required to conduct studies on existing drugs, safety, and effectiveness in for children.

Incidents like these forced Congress to create laws and the FDA to step out of its comfort zone and expand regulatory control over drugs, cosmetics, therapeutic devices, and computer systems. These deaths and deformities have resulted in the promulgation of new regulations

---

[34] (Sulfanilamide disaster, 2015)

controlling the introduction of medicines into the marketplace. The FDA requires that drugs be proven safe before they are introduced into the marketplace and the tolerance limits are to be set on products to avoid poisoning people. Within the drug enforcement domain is the ability to take immediate action against those companies or individuals who misbrand products. Enforcement actions include factory inspections, court injunctions, seizures, and prosecutions. The mission of the FDA is to enforce laws enacted by the U.S. Congress and regulations established by the FDA to protect the consumer's safety.

Laws & Guidance's

FDA Guidance's are documents that explain FDA's position on a subject. They also include minor changes in the agency's interpretation of topics and changes in the FDA policy, that are related to regulatory issues. The FDA uses guidance to guide entities on best practices. Guidance not only addresses the design, manufacturing, testing maintenance, monitoring, and reporting of regulated products, but it also includes the FDA's current thinking on scientific issues, inspections, and enforcement policies. Although guidance are not legally binding, they clarify the FDA's position on specific topics. If the FDA shares advice on how computer systems are to function within a regulated environment, it makes sense to follow their line of reasoning, especially if it relates to information systems, products, and services that are within its regulatory jurisdiction.

Electronic Records; Electronic Signatures (21 CFR Part 11) is a guidance document created by the FDA to explain the agency's stance on what security measures should be in place for systems that house electronic records and utilize signatures. 21 CFR Part 11 was created not only for companies who host regulated electronic records but for use by the FDA's internal staff. This security guidance document speaks to the design, validation, and verification of computerized systems used to facilitate the production of products, services, and aid in developing the scientific rational behind issues associated with goods and services. 21 CFR Part 11 does not explicitly call out Cloud computing, but it does speak to the design and architecture of computer systems that are supporting regulated records. For systems that are used in regulated spaces, it speaks to how a system is to be validated to ensure consistent performance within a controlled environment, electronic records that are being managed by the system, and the minimum controls that must be in place to provide consistent performance.

Section 21 of the Code of Federal Regulations (CFR) Part 820, which is referred to as Quality System regulation QSR. It contains the Food and

Drug Administration's (FDA) current thinking on a company's Quality System (Organization).

The QS regulation[35] applies to finished device manufacturers who intend to commercially distribute medical devices. A finished device is defined in 21 CFR 820.3(l) as any device or accessory to any device that is suitable for use or capable of functioning, whether or not it is packaged, labeled, or sterilized. For the purposes of this book, we refer to devices that contain one or more software components, parts, or accessories, or are composed solely of software as "software devices," including:

1. firmware and other means for software-based control of medical devices
2. stand-alone software applications
3. software intended for installation in general-purpose computers
4. dedicated hardware/software medical devices.
5. accessories to medical devices when those accessories contain or are composed of software.

QSR are formalized business practices that define management responsibilities for organizational structure, processes, procedures and resources needed to fulfill product/service requirements, customer satisfaction, and continual improvement. QSR speaks to the minimum controls that must be in place to satisfy the agency. Regulatory authorities require companies who handle Pharmaceutical, Healthcare and Medical Device electronic information to manage activities that may affect the integrity of the data. Each documented activity in regulated space

---

[35] (Center, Health, and Evaluation, 2016)

generates a record. Most records are created from raw data collected by computer technology using some combination of hardware and software. After records are created someone of authority verifies or approves the information and process. A system that provides management oversight for the creation and management of information from creation through its retention period is called the Quality System.

The FDA has also established a set of Good Manufacturing Practices (GMPs), Good Clinical Practices (GCPs), Good Laboratory Practices (GLPs) and Good Documentation Practices (GDPs) for the food and drug arena. We call these practices (GXPs) or Predicate Rules because they are the theory of structure upon which later laws and guidelines was predicated. GXPs are not difficult to understand. They make good business sense. The funny thing is, that most businesses may be already be operating using industry best practices but do not know it. They may have some statistical process in place that's based on sound science. The processes may not be as prescriptive as written in the GXP but it provides consumers with the utmost quality. Most companies have integrated some form of best practices into their business model that allows them to produce quality products and services. Most computer systems have security characteristics that when properly configured could easily meet regulatory requirements. If you are providing reputable products and services, you probably already have some form of quality practices built into your business processes. A Gap Assessment or Risk Assessment will help you determine if existing computerized systems meet FDA's best practices and industry standards. The assessment will also provide visibility into high-risk activities and give you the opportunity to develop a mitigation strategy. FDA's GXPs[36] are:

1. Current Good Manufacturing Practices (cGMP): cGMP are a set of regulations, codes, and guidelines governing the manufacture of drug substances, drug products, medical devices, in vivo (in the living body of a plant or animal), in vitro (taking place in a test tube, culture dish, or elsewhere outside a living organism) diagnostic products, and foods.

2. Current Good Clinical Practices (cGCP): cGCP are a set of regulations, codes, and guidelines governing the design, conduct, performance, monitoring, auditing, recording, analysis and reporting of clinical trials or clinical studies.

3. Current Good Laboratory Practice (cGLP): cGLPs are a set of regulations governing nonclinical laboratory studies that support products regulated by the FDA Food and Drug Administration, including food and color additives, animal food additives, human and animal drugs, and medical devices for human use, biological products, and electronic products. This experimentation is usually completed on animals.

4. Current Good Documentation Practices (cGDP): cGDP is an expected practice and not a federal requirement. You can find a few references in the Medical Device Quality Systems) manual (Section 9) and ICH Q7A (Section IV-A).

---

[36] (Dent, 1996)

Regulatory oversight is not just limited to ensuring validation of IT systems; it also includes jurisdiction over the data managed by these systems and management oversight of the system. The FDA monitors and regulates drug development processes around the world. Its role in the pre-clinical research stage (GLP) is not limited to evaluating data collected from research, but ensuring that the research was properly executed. This includes having oversight over detailed documentation that supports pre-clinical research and development. The FDA gives a favorable pre-clinical standing to companies who follow Good Laboratory Practices. Once a company finds sufficient evidence that a drug is successful when it is administered to animals, it will initiate human testing. Moving from an investigational new drug to testing in humans requires the efforts of professionals from many disciplines. Companies use GCPs when considering drug testing in humans. A new drug application can be filed with the FDA after multiple phases of clinical trials have been proven successful. Companies must demonstrate that a drug product is safe and effective. The product must also correlate with its purported quality. It must clearly demonstrate that it is paralleled to what is stated on the label. Lastly, it must be manufactured in an environment that utilizes good practices. Good Manufacturing practices described manufacturing techniques that are acceptable to the FDA. The pharmaceutical company must be able to demonstrate that the new drug product can be manufactured successfully. This includes proving that its computerized systems are functioning as intended.

The FDA will review a company's electronic and paper records to determine if a company is following GLPs, GCPs, and GMPs. The review will include a consideration of the companies documentation standards utilizing Good Documentation Practices GDPs. GDPs must be thoroughly integrated into a company's business and reporting practices. Recordkeeping practices are heavily scrutinized by the agency. GLPs, GCPs, and GMPs are essential tools for determining the drug's effectiveness, quality, purity, and safety. If a firm does not establish GDPs, communicating scientific results can be extremely difficult. GLPs, GCPs, GDPs, and GMPs are used to get drug products approved for use in the marketplace. During this process, millions of electronic and paper records are generated in order to gain one product approval.

The healthcare industry's goal is not to manage redundant cumbersome computer systems and networks. Managing massive amounts of information is not within their core competency. Cloud computing is a viable option for regulated industries. It gives Healthcare companies more time to focus on developing safe and effective products instead of managing old outdated computer systems. Cloud computing makes sense for research and development, clinical trial management, post-marketing studies, saleable products, operations, patient care, etc.

There are approximately two hundred seventy-four references to how entities in the regulatory space are expected to manage electronic records, computers, documentation, software and approvals in the following regulations. It is important to know these laws and guidance if you plan to do work in the regulatory space. Why is it that we have focused on these five terms to drive the importance of regulations? Well, it's because they are the critical points of action for the information lifecycle.

Term	**Regulations**			
	QSR (Pt820)	**GLP (Pt58)**	**GMP (Pt211)**	**ER/ES (Pt11)**
Computer ≈	2	1	7	7
Software ≈	7	0	0	1
Records ≈	53	30	18	82
Documentation ≈	11	9	4	21
Approvals ≈	11	3	7	1

1. Computer: The agency wants to be assured with a high degree of certainty that your computerized system will function as intended and that it ensures data confidentiality, privacy, security, integrity, authenticity, reliability, legibility, and data availability.

2. Software: The agency wants to be assured that your software was developed under a defined and reliable Software Development Lifecycle (SDLC) process.

3. Records: The agency wants to make sure that the conditions under which raw data is identified sorted and compiled into a record and managed is reliable and proven.

4. Documentation: Documentation must be scientifically driven and presented in a rational format that's clear understandable and accessible within a reasonable time

5. Approvals: The agency wants well-defined authority checks and approvals by an independent qualified personal for all of the above. The Quality Assurance Unit (QUA) provides an independent approvals.

If you have the above basis covered, you've just rounded first base. When assessing your computer system, you must take into consideration the impact these five words have on your processes. If controls for computer systems are not in place, you can open up yourself to serious scrutiny. Youll, see these words crop up over and over again as we begin to delve into the laws, guidances, policies, and standards.

Good Documentation Practices

Good Documentation Practices should be interpreted the same way for Good Clinical Practices and Good Manufacturing Practices and receive no less scrutiny. In this case, the internal and external systems must be tested to ensure that it possesses the same technical, procedural, policies, and management controls. Documentation supporting design and testing must be readily accessible to regulatory authorities in a reasonable period. The retention period is the time that a record must be kept. At the end of the retention period, a record can be discarded unless there is a Document Preservation Notice in place related to the record. Courts may view the improper destruction of records as a deliberate attempt to obstruct justice or conceal harmful information. Due to the varying legal restraints within countries, record retention times differ. It is important that the SLA contain language surrounding migration, transformation, and destruction of documents.

Phase	Description	GXP Data
GDP All above phases	Applied to all reports	Applicable To All of the Above

Hysteria hits many companies when audit teams scour through their record retention and destruction practices. They scour through paper boxes for records, e-mail , backup tapes, and such, to find evidence of past activities. Historically, record retention is expensive and inefficient. If not done correctly, a host of legal challenges could open. Retaining and discarding information must be completed in a methodical fashion. A complimentary document retention program that is based on statutory or regulatory record-keeping requirements should:

1. include a risk analysis; an assessment needs to be completed on (tax records, bookkeeping, and insurance, property, and personnel records) for investigators, etc.
2. Not comprise of relevant information to the company's activities

3. Be driven by specific requirements and not by the need to collect everything
4. provide cataloguing and easy access for the regulatory agencies
5. Be proceduralized

Record retention can be an expensive proposition. Retrieving records from a mismanaged catalog system can be very costly. The simple act of retrieving records from a mismanaged company is costly, in and of itself.

Global Marketplace

W We're in a global marketplace. As a result of sweeping economic and technological changes, international trade has increased throughout the United States. This increase has revolutionized the way in which goods and services are shared around the world. Professionals within the healthcare industry have immediate access to drugs and medical devices developed in different locations. Consumers around the world enjoy access to products and services that have not been accessible because of locality. An ever-flowing broader selection of goods and services, Who has never seen before, are presented by globalization. The trade of this magnitude has resulted in a host of government statutory and regulatory requirements, services and agencies as well as international institutions being put in place to help manage the world's rapidly growing needs. The regulatory agencies regulates products that are used around the world.

The regulatory agencies play a substantial role in the global economy. Food and drug products, their ingredients and components, and products that directly and profoundly affect the health and welfare of the public are increasingly being sourced from abroad. The FDA has one of the largest databases in the world. The FDA relies on Cloud networking to manage most of these activities. Currently, the FDA is holding food importers responsible for the verification of their requirements. Merchants must meet the same safety requirements as domestic suppliers One mishap in paperwork or computer system failure can cause the deaths of thousands of people. The need to develop a knowledge-sharing culture becomes extremely critical as we move into a more complex regulatory environment. Sharing technical expertise with foreign regulatory counterparts enhances a country's ability to produce safe and effective products. Sound leadership and a strong infrastructure are a necessity. Exchange of information helps foreign countries enhance their regulatory infrastructure, safeguard the health of their citizens, and contribute to their global health.

Global GXPs (Best Practices)

Best practices have been codified into the Code of Federal regulations and regulated by the executive branch of the US government. GXPs or best practices are recognized worldwide. GXPs are one of the most controversial legal documents the FDA has created. However, Guidance's are not enforceable by law. FDA Guidance's contain the FDA's current thinking on a particular topic and should be viewed as recommendations. However, if you were to deviate from a guidance would it require a strong scientific argument. The FDA is in the business of reviewing scientific information and not creating valid science.

The FDA is not the global police. It does not have the resources to police how companies achieve quality, purity, and efficacy. The FDA collaborates with organizations who are aligned with its goals. Regulatory agencies develop partnerships with various standards organizations to help govern activities and promote good science in the industry. There are hundreds of professional organizations that have established quality standards or well-defined practices for conducting laboratory testing, manufacturing processes, formulating materials, and computer development. Regulatory agencies reference the efforts of these reputable standards organizations that they believe provide good science.

The United States (US), Japan, European Union (EU) and Australia are not the only entities that have GXPs. Organizations like the Economic Co-operation and Development (OECD), a European Economic Development company has its version of GXPs. OECD is neither a legal nor a political entity. Nevertheless, it has been established for the purpose of establishing good practices for its members. Merging GXPs is a strategic decision to reduce the cost associated with product testing, design, and specifications, product launches, regulatory approval, etc. By merging GXPs, entities can perform testing under one protocol for acceptance in multiple economies. This saves time and money.

As the regulatory community moves to centralize its efforts, companies can launch a plethora of products and services under one regulating body. Earlier in the chapter we have been looking at GXPs from a drug development lens, but GXPs are not limited to the healthcare arena. Governments can create their set of regional practices. US, Japan, Australia have their GXPs. Political bodies can develop local practices. The European Union has eliminated the British, Nordic, and German GXPs and it has created a set of GXPs that represent that's representative of the European Union practices. Industrial monopolies have the muscle to establish Good Practices. OECD has a set of practices for high income producing countries. Countries can harmonize or merge GXPs.

The US, Japan, and EU have combined GXPs into a set of practices. These combined practices are called International Conference on Harmonization (ICH). Europe, Middle East, and Africa (business/market areas) (EMEA) has had mutual recognition of a specific set of GXPs with Japan and Canada. Here are some best practices or industry-accepted standards

Asia-Pacific Economic Cooperation (APEC)

APEC[37] is the premier Asia-Pacific economic forum. APECs primary goal is to support sustainable economic growth and prosperity in the Asia-Pacific region. APEC has developed a blend of best practices in the form of a blended approach of voluntary, co-regulatory and legislative regulatory mechanisms undertaken in partnership between governments. APEC has 21 members. The word *economies* is used to describe APEC members because the APEC cooperative process is predominantly concerned with trade and economic issues, with members engaging with one another as economic entities. The goal of the organization is to improve behind-the-border barriers to trade. APEC has been working to foster transparency, competition and better functioning markets in the Asia-Pacific through regulatory reform, improving public sector and corporate governance, and strengthening the legal infrastructure. Since 2004, APEC has implemented

[37] (Bendebka and Hossain, 2012)

predictable and transparent regulatory practices across the region. For example, APEC members have made great strides in ensuring new government laws are publicly communicated, and their cost and benefits are appropriately assessed. Why does the ASEAN relationship matter to the FDA? There is a greater likelihood that food will be exposed to pathogens, contaminants or chemical hazards during a journey of this complexity. That's why we work closely with our regional counterparts in these countries through such organizations as the Association of Southeast Asian Nations (ASEAN), sharing with them regulatory requirements, and knowledge of good manufacturing practices and our laboratory and inspection techniques. Through such information sharing, we can prevent tainted or otherwise unsafe foods from reaching our borders

In 2007, a Data Privacy Pathfinder initiative was established to progress the implementation of the APEC Privacy Framework. The Pathfinder involves multiple projects aimed at promoting consumer trust and business confidence in cross-border data flows. It also includes general commitments regarding the development of a Cross-Border Privacy Rules system toward creation of a Privacy Enforcement Authority for enforcing Cross-Border Privacy Rules

Association of the Southeast Asian Nations (ASEAN)

ASEAN[38] was formed in 1967. The Association of Southeast Asian Nations (ASEAN) is an alliance promoting economic and political cooperation by fostering dialogue among its ten members: Brunei, Cambodia, Indonesia, Laos, Malaysia, Myanmar, the Philippines, Singapore,

---

[38] (von Feigenblatt, 2012)

Thailand, and Vietnam. ASEAN is becoming a major economic powerhouse in the region, having signed free-trade agreements (FTA) with China, Australia, New Zealand, India, Japan, and Korea. The ASEAN Community is comprised of three pillars, the Political-Security Community, Economic Community and Socio-Cultural Community

Association of Southeast Asian Nations Pharmaceutical Product Working Group (ASEAN PPWG) was established in 1999 by the ACCSQ (ASEAN Consultative Committee for Standards and Quality).The mission of the PPWG is to develop harmonization schemes of pharmaceutical regulations of the ASEAN Member countries to complement and facilitate the objective of AFTA (ASEAN Free Trade Area), particularly, the elimination of technical barriers to trade posed by regulations, without compromising on drug quality, efficacy, and safety.

Gulf Cooperation Council (GCC)

The Gulf Cooperation Council [GCC][39] was established in an agreement concluded on 25 May 1981 in Riyadh, Saudi Arabia between Bahrain, Kuwait, Oman, Qatar, Saudi Arabia and UAE. These countries declared that the GCC is established in view of the special relations between them, their similar political systems based on Islamic beliefs, joint destiny, and common objectives. The GCC is a regional common market with a defense planning council as well. The

[39] (Al-Mubaraki et al., 2013)

geographic proximity of these countries and their general adoption of free trade economic policies are factors that encouraged them to establish the GCC.

The GCC Gulf Cooperation Council is focusing its energies on developing joint ventures that will encourage cooperation by from the private sector for the good of their peoples. The council is striving to induce advanced stages of economic integration towards the development of a common market and an economic and monetary Union among member states. These goals are driven by rigid timetables that enforce market mechanisms and foster the role of the private sector. This interconnection of countries will strengthen their relationship and establish a central area for coordination, integration, and interconnection in all fields of study. It will stimulate cooperation between their peoples in various areas. This interconnection will harmonize their economic, financial and monetary policies, their commercial and industrial laws, as well as their customs and regulations.

Pan American Network for Drug Regulatory Harmonization (PANDRH)

PANDRH[40] constitutes a continental forum on drug regulatory harmonization. Pan American Network promotes drug regulatory harmonization for the quality, safety, and efficacy of pharmaceutical products that will enhance the quality of life and health care of the citizens of the Member Countries of the Americas. PANDRH constitutes a continental forum on drug regulatory harmonization. PANDRH was

[40] (Mitchell, 2016)

officially established in November 1999, with official recognition by the 42nd Directing Council of the Pan American Health Organization (PAHO) in September 2000. PANDRH's scope of harmonization/cooperative activities includes technical guidelines, regulatory processes and the strengthening of national regulatory agencies through harmonization of processes and standards to improve drug quality and quality assurance.

Specific drug sectors covered include prescription, over the counter, generics, 'similars', biologics/vaccines and herbal medicines. Its purpose is to provide requirements for establishing regulations and regulatory tools that will contribute to the harmonization process of medicines registration to ensuring the efficacy, quality and safety of medicines to be available in the countries of our Region. It was officially established in 1999.

Core country participants in PANDRH include Mexico, Costa Rica, Trinidad and Tobago, Argentina, and Colombia. Its alternates include United States, Panama, Barbados, Chile, and Bolivia. PANDH is comprised of various working groups: GMP, GCP, pharmacopeia, pharmacovigilance, GLP, vaccines, etc. PANDH has established a series of technical guidelines and documents that govern:

1. GMP Inspections
2. Good Clinical Practices
3. Labeling And Patent Information
4. Drug Counterfeiting
5. Classification Of Over-The-Counter Drugs

---

[41] (Muntschick, 2017)

Southern African Development Community (SADC)

SADC[41] is a regional economic community comprising of fifteen state members; Angola, Botswana, Democratic Republic of Congo, Lesotho, Madagascar, Malawi, Mauritius, Mozambique, Namibia, Seychelles, South Africa, Swaziland, Tanzania, Zambia, and Zimbabwe. Established in 1992, SADC is committed to regional integration and poverty eradication within Southern Africa through economic development and ensuring peace and security. The primary objectives of SADC are to

1. Harmonizing treatment guidelines and medicine lists
2. Create regional pharmaceutical opportunities by maximizing research and development
3. Strengthening the capacity supply and of distributing pharmaceutical products by making pharmaceutical products more affordable and available
4. Encourage joint procurement to ensure that safe, effective, and quality driven products are more affordable and acceptable

On 12 June, 2011, the Heads of State and Government of the Common Market for Eastern and Southern Africa (COMESA), the East African Community (EAC) and the Southern African Development community (SADC) met and signed a declaration launching negotiations for the establishment of the COMESA-EAC-SADC Free Trade Area (FTA). The Common Market for COMESA-EAC-SADC comprises 26 countries with a combined population of nearly 600 million people and a total Gross Domestic Product (GDP) of approximately US$1.0 trillion. The primary objective of the COMESA-EAC-SADC Tripartite is strengthening and deepening the economic integration of the southern and eastern Africa region. This will be achieved through harmonization of policies and programs across the three Regional Economic Communities (RECs) in the areas of trade, customs, and infrastructure development.

International Harmonization Guidelines (ICH)

ICH[42] guidelines are enforced and cited by FDA, EMA, Health Canada, and other health agencies involved in international regulatory harmonization efforts. The Global Harmonization Task Force (GHTF) was founded in 1993 by the governments and industry representatives of Australia, Canada, Japan, the European Union, and the United States of America. The purpose of the GHTF is to encourage a convergence in standards and regulatory practices related to the safety, performance, and quality of medical devices. The GHTF also promotes technological innovation and facilitates international trade. The primary means by which its goals are accomplished is via the publication and dissemination of harmonized guidance documents for basic regulatory practices. GHTF could facilitate access for developing countries (both those importing and those wishing to manufacture) to provide Information on the major regulatory systems for medical device approvals and health technology assessment and the adoption of a single medical device nomenclature

1. ICH Global Harmonization Task Force (GHTF) section SG3.N17 is guidance on quality management systems, medical devices, and

---

[42] (Mentions, 2017)

advice on the control of products and services that are obtained from suppliers. A Guidance on Quality Management System – Medical Devices – Guidance on the Control of Products and Services Obtained from Suppliers:

2. ICH Global Harmonization Task Force (GHTF) section SG3.N99 of GHTF is the guidance for quality systems for the design and manufacturing of medical devices. Guidance On Quality Systems For The Design And Manufacture Of Medical Devices. This document provides general guidance on the implementation of quality systems for medical devices based on ISO 9001.
3. ICH E6 Good Clinical Practice: Are a Consolidated Guidance Strict requirements surrounding Trial Management, Data Handling, Recordkeeping, and Independent Data Monitoring Committee. The sponsor may consider establishing an independent data monitoring committee (IDMC).
4. ICH Q7 Guidance: Good Manufacturing Practice Guide For Active Pharmaceutical Ingredients is guidance. This document (Guide) is intended to provide guidance regarding good manufacturing practice (GMP) for the production of active pharmaceutical ingredients (APIs) under an appropriate system for managing quality. It is also intended to help ensure that APIs meet the requirements for quality and purity that they purport or are represented to possess.

AS ISO 15489 Australian Standard on Records Management

A records management standard that was launched in October 2001, at the Association of Records Management and Administrator's

(ARMA)[43] International Conference in Montreal. The standard was developed by an international committee and is strongly based on the record management of Australian standards. SO 15489 was designed to meet the ongoing generic needs for recordkeeping in a business environment and was intended to have a universal application. Issued in 2002 by both the International Standards organization and Standards Australia. AS ISO 15489 Australian Standard on Records Management has become the benchmark standard for developing and implementing recordkeeping systems. The standard has two parts. ISO 15489 Part 1[44] of ISO 15489 presents the I framework for recordkeeping. It explains the benefits of good records management, along with the legal considerations that emphasize the responsibility of recordkeeping and the importance of making someone responsible for recordkeeping.

This part also looks at what's needed for proper records management, Included in the ISO 15489 are designing recordkeeping systems, records management processes, auditing, and training. ISO 15489 Part 2: Guideline is a guide for placing Part 1's advice into practice for putting the information given in Part 1 into practice. It provides specific details on developing records management policy and responsibility statements on how to develop policies and declarations concerning responsibility and suggests a process for developing for recordkeeping systems.

It also provides advice about improving records processes and controls such as thesauri, disposal authorities, and security and access

---

[43] (AS ISO 15489 Australian standard on records management, 2017)
[44] (Institution and Institute, 2001)

arrangements. It discusses how you might use these tools the tools might be used to manage your records (including capturing, registering, classifying and storing). It also gives specific advice about setting up monitoring, auditing and training programs are also offered.

Chapter 4

Electronic Record Keeping

GXPs are written to ensure that products are safe, meet their intended use, and in regulated industries adhere to quality processes during manufacturing, control, storage and distribution. In addition to GXPs, FDA guidance 21 CFR Part 11 (Electronic Records and Signatures)[45],

[45] (Guidance for industry part 11, electronic records; electronic signatures — scope and application, 2003)

and EU's Annex 11 are guides to support computer security. If a company is complying with these guidelines, it is fulfilling some of the FDA's requirements for computerized systems used in healthcare areas. FDA guidance 21 CFR Part 11 Electronic records and electronic signatures and EU's Annex 11 are a sure bet for strengthening your computer systems security. With the advent of Cloud Computing, there is a fundamental shift in the way that healthcare providers are storing data. Information that is searched, shared, and collected within the GXP environment is creating new venues for which clinical development and data sharing can take place. As a matter of fact, Cloud Computing presents new challenges for regulatory agencies. Regulatory activity surrounding the adoption of cloud computing in the healthcare, pharmaceutical, chemical, medical device, hospital, and the biotechnology environment are not as forthcoming as some would like to see. However, there are numerous laws and guidance on how computerized systems should be used in the regulated space. Companies are moving to the Cloud in record numbers. Regardless of the perceived regulatory risks associated with Cloud Computing, the hook has been cast, and businesses are biting. The speed of acceptance is alarming. Data is being migrated into the Cloud from numerous computerized systems.

Cloud networks must be assessed for risk to ensure that the conditions under which information is processed and collected ensures data confidentiality, privacy, security, integrity, authenticity, reliability, legibility, and data availability and that computerized system will perform as intended with a high degree of certainty. Also, that documentation is clear understandable and accessible within a reasonable period, and software is developed under a defined SDLC process with well-defined authority checks and approvals by an independent qualified personal.

Each GXP practice has its unique computerized systems requirements. With this uniqueness comes a set of management controls that are unique to that data (GXP). These controls must be in place to ensure the integrity of records and the reliability of the process. Management controls (training, procedures, audits, change management, risk management, metrics, etc.) at the SP are expected to have the same or a greater level of integrity and rigor than at the client's site. Also, security Practices are supposed to restrict user access to regulated information, and procedural controls should define the roles and responsibilities needed to operate and maintain integrity in the environment.

In August 1997, the FDA's regulations on electronic signatures and electronic records became effective. 21 CFR Part 11 Security, describes the technical and procedural requirements that must be met if a firm chooses to maintain records electronically and uses electronic signatures. Part 11 works in conjunction with other FDA regulations and laws that require recordkeeping.

Most firms do not understand the regulatory requirements governing information in their possession. They have have controlled access but do not understand what they should be protecting. They are good at developing security measures but lousy at privacy. Thus making regulated information exposed. Without this understanding, how can anyone accurately assess the risk and appropriately develop mitigation strategies? An assessment helps determine if a firm's quality systems are adequately resourced to manage company information. Electronic information is not equal. Specialized data cannot be secured by technical controls alone. Systems administrators must ensure that procedural controls be developed to instruct employees on how to process unique information. Most regulatory agencies require companies to establish and maintain records throughout the product or service lifecycle. Whether you are working with financial records, investigations, CAPA or in manufacturing, processing, transporting or distributing, each undertaking must have the ability to process, identify, store, maintain, retain and retire records, documents, procedures, contracts, and everything about the recording system. Not only are cloud systems essential towards generating electronic records, but they are extremely critical for maintaining and tracking document generation throughout the products' lifecycle.

Types of Data Generated in Healthcare Environments

Regulated companies are looking for ways of obtaining and maintaining approvals for their products in the most efficient way possible.There is a significant gulf between where organizations need to be and where they are today. Cloud computing offers the value and flexibility that can companies speed up product development, simplify data exchange. Tracking regulatory information is no easy task. Recent improvements in cloud technologies have led to more sophisticated services that feature enhanced security and a quicker path to successful regulatory compliance. Cloud-based document management services allows you to create a lean organization with more dynamic processes that can quickly adapt to regulatory changes. It reduces day-to-day management overhead and allows an organization to be agiler and to ramp up initiatives incredibly fast. Despite pressure from the authorities to abide by new rules governing data capture, just a fraction of healthcare companies has fully implemented a global strategy for regulatory information management for tracking regulatory information. Information managers need to ensure their regulatory records are managed successfully in all countries where they operate.

Records required by CGMP regulations must designed and maintained by the originating company. Because the CGMP regulations provide considerable latitude on how these requirements are to be achieved, manufacturers are allowed to establish their methods of recordkeeping. FDA accepts any electronic recordkeeping system which meets the objectives of the 21 CFR Part 211[46]. Manufacturing establishments may use automated, mechanical, or electronic devices or any type of equipment, including computers, or related systems that can meet regulatory requirements within a specific degree of confidence.

---

[46] (CFR 2011 title21 vol4 part211, 2014)

Computer tapes, microfiche, or microfilm or copies may be used instead of hard copy records to collect, retrieve and store information. The Food and Drug Administration (FDA) Current good Manufacturing Practice (CGMP) Regulations for Finished Pharmaceuticals (21 CFR Part 211) requires drug manufacturers to establish and maintain quality control procedures for manufacturing, processing and holding drugs and drug products. FDA has determined that these information requirements be essential to meeting the agency's statutory responsibility for protecting public safety and health. FDA oversees the following information collection requirements in the CGMP regulations (21 CFR Part 211) For more CGMP recordkeeping requirements.

211.34
211.67
211.68
211.68(a)
211.68(b)
211.72 4
211.80(d)
211.100(b)

211.105(b)
211.122
211.130(e)
211.132
211.132(d)
211.137
2111.160(a)
211.165
211.166
211.173
211.180(e)

211.180(f)
211.182
211.184
211.186
211.188
211.192
211.194
211.196
211.198
211.204

IT solutions are the means for which drug development can be processed. The IT value chain extends to Drug discovery and development, animal studies, clinical trials, manufacturing, quality-control, enterprise resource planning, supply chain managements, business intelligence, data warehousing, enterprise applications, and management. Facilities Utilities and Equipment: Facilities utilities and equipment have a direct impact on the safety, identify, potency-strength, quality, or purity of the product. They directly impact regulatory aspects of the manufacturing process. Facility utilities and equipment are used to maintain, control, and monitor environmental conditions to preserve product quality. They are also used to clean, sanitize, or sterilize to maintain product quality. Some examples of GMP-critical F/E/U include bottle/cap molding machines, filtered compressed air, ISO 5 cleanrooms, and inspection systems. Data collected from the Facilities utilities and equipment is fed into the Electronic Database Management System (EDMS). The EDMS is a collection of technologies that works collectively to provide a comprehensive solution for managing the creation, capture, indexing, storage, retrieval, and disposition of records and information assets of an organization. Below are some typically regulated documentation likely seen within the healthcare arena. The list is not exhaustive, but it'll give you a good idea.

1. Engineering drawings and reports for: equipment, systems, building automation systems, building communication systems, purified water systems, compressed gas systems, building security systems, process systems, instrumentation & control systems,

mechanical/HVAC systems, electrical systems, pest control systems, fire protection systems, plumbing systems, utilities systems, environmental monitoring system

2. Annual product review, yearly trending, and metrics report changing control assessments
3. Batch control records, logbooks, research and development diaries
4. Bills of lading
5. Records, alarms, monitoring, etc., from various control systems such as BAS, BMS, SCADA, EMS, HVAC, etc.
6. Calibration records operation & maintenance records.
7. Certificate of analyses
8. Change controls
9. Chemical analysis, component specifications, analytical specifications and methods for raw materials, molecular formulas, chemical dispositions and disposals, inventories
10. Cleaning and sanitization records
11. Cleaning logbooks
12. Clinical file dossiers, clinical studies, clinical research, clinical trial records, management for trial drug supplies, clinical trial, records maintained by investigators.
13. Commercial stability
14. Consumer complaints
15. Contracts/Agreements
16. Copy clearance manuscripts
17. Corrective actions/preventative maintenance
18. Employee personnel records and consultant files
19. Engineering drawings: such as plant layout, personnel, material, waste, cleanliness
20. Environmental monitoring records
21. Facility access and security authorization records
22. FDA field alert, regulatory inquiries, correspondences, market actions,
23. Checklists and service records.
24. Formulations, formulation numbers, master formula

profiles, molecular formulas, chemical titles, active ingredients, pharmaceutical titles

25. GLP studies
26. Hazardous material inventory and waste manifests
27. Health and safety files, daily exposure testing, Air emissions sampling and permits
28. Information management
29. Inspection reports
30. Invention disclosures names, ideas, subjects, chemical name.
31. Investigation reports
32. Laboratory, facilities, utilities, manufacturing and packaging equipment, devices, instrumentation, logbooks, work orders, reports for maintenance, commissioning and qualification, calibration, validation (cleaning, CSV, product, process, etc.,.)
33. Maintenance logs
34. Medical device control releases notifications, management, regulatory activities, implants, post-market surveillances, and adverse event files.
35. Non-conformances, deviations, excursions, corrective actions (preventive maintenance), cause analysis,
36. Patents and applications
37. Permits and Certifications
38. Pest control logs
39. Physical inventory assessments
40. Policies and procedures
41. Product recalls, NDA field alerts, recalls
42. Research reports, studies
43. Retain samples, return goods/ destruct authorizations, return to vendor forms, complaint product history, product review sheets,
44. Risk analyses, for compliances, regulatory, business, product, etc,
45. Sales forecasts
46. Scientific publications, secrecy agreements
47. Security Logs
48. SOX requirements

49. Specifications for raw materials, products, packages, equipment, designs, functional, analytical, methods, etc.
50. Stability reports
51. Standard operating procedures
52. Training materials, records, documentation, curricula
53. Transference of documentations
54. Trial master file clinical trial participants.

"I'm in a paperwork mood, let 'er rip."

Record keeping legislation

Electronic record keeping is not just a GXP phenomenon. The federal government has a Crockpot of legislation for determining:

1. What records must be maintained
2. How long must the records be retained
3. Where the records must be maintained
4. What are requirements for making the record available
5. What procedures does the agency intend to follow before requesting access to records

6. How to request copies of your records
7. How to maintain the confidentiality of any protected information
8. Determining what will happen if the required records are not established and maintained

Here are just some of the legislation requirements governing information.

Bioterrorism Act of 2002[47]

This act requires the establishment and maintenance of records by persons who manufacture, process, pack, transport, distribute, receive, hold or import food in the United States. Companies who engage in the above activities must establish a process whereby records are serviced. This includes but not limited to assessing the storage of files for adequate retention times, filing schemes and document repository. The requirement to establish and maintain records is one of the several tools that will help improve FDA's ability to respond to, and further contain, threats of severe adverse health consequences or death to humans or animals from accidental or deliberate contamination of food. As a responsible official of a facility that manufactures/processes, packs, or holds food for human or animal consumption in the United States, you are responsible for ensuring that your overall operation and the products you distribute are in compliance with the law.

---

[47] (Commissioner, 2014)

Federal Food, Drug and Cosmetic Act (FDCA)[48]

The expectation is that companies exporting records be maintained for the same period of time as required for records subject to retention requirement by regulatory requirements that are applicable to the product. The records shall be made available to the Food and Drug Administration (FDA), upon request, during an inspection for review and copying by FDA. Records that are needed to assist FDA in determining whether the food is adulterated and presents a threat of serious adverse health consequences or death to humans or animals to determine where there is a reasonable probability that the use of or exposure to the food will cause serious adverse health consequences or death to human or animals. Records include but are not limited to:

- Manufacturing records
- Raw materials (ingredients and packaging) receipt records
- Product distribution records
- Product inventory records
- Test records
- Recall records
- Reportable food records
- Customer distribution lists
- Complaint and adverse event records

Prescription Drug Marketing Act (PDMA)[49]

The PDMA, which was signed by the president on April 22, 1988, was enacted to ensure that prescription drug products purchased by consumers would be safe and effective and to avoid an

---

[48] (Commissioner, 2016)
[49] (carolyn.becker, 2006)

unacceptable risk that counterfeit, adulterated, misbranded, sub-potent or expired drugs were being sold to the American public. Congress decided that legislation was necessary because there were insufficient safeguards in the prescription drug distribution system to prevent the introduction and retail sale of substandard, ineffective, or counterfeit drugs and that a wholesale drug diversion submarket had developed that prevented effective control over, or even routine knowledge of, the right sources of drugs.

PDMA requires state licensing of wholesale distributors of prescription drugs; requires unauthorized wholesale distributors to provide purchasers a statement (also called a pedigree) identifying each prior sale of the drug. PDMA requires A list of the specific products that the wholesale distributor is authorized to distribute or a statement that the wholesale distributor is an Authorized Distributor of Record (ADR) for the manufacturer's entire product line. Specific products should be identified by the name, dosage form, and strength of the drug, or the NDC number; and shall retain them for at least three years after the date of their creation.

The pedigree is subject to the record federal retention requirements and must be retained by all wholesale distributors involved in the distribution of the drug product, whether ADR or non-ADR, for three years. FDA encourages pharmacies and other end users to retain the pedigree for three years. As a result, if there is any question about the source or history of the product, it can be traced back through the drug supply chain.

Information regarding "each prior transaction involving the drug, starting with the manufacture" must be included in the pedigree. However, for injunction purposes, the pedigrees should include information regarding prior transactions going back to the manufacturer or the last ADR that sold, purchased, or traded the prescription drugs. FDA encourages wholesalers to include information regarding each prior transaction going back to the manufacturer when that information is available.

Food and Drug Administration Amendments Act of 2007 (FDAAA)[50]

Food Drug and Cosmetic Act (FD&C) requires the establishment of a Reportable Food Registry (the Registry) by which instances of reportable food must be submitted to FDA by responsible parties and may be submitted by public health officials. If a federal, state or local public health official identifies a reportable food as part of the inspection or regulatory activities, can the public health official inform the facility that they may be required to submit a report?

Whatever your role, (manufacturer, health care professional, researcher, public health official, or concerned citizen), the FDA will examine or inspect my records related to reports received, notifications made, and reports submitted to FDA. The responsible party shall maintain records related to each report received, notification made, and report submitted to the FDA.

---

[50] (Commissioner, 2015)

FD&C Act requires that responsible persons maintain records related to reportable foods reports and notifications for two years. It defines "reportable food" as an "article of food (other than infant formula) for which there is a reasonable probability that the use of, or exposure to, such article of food will cause serious adverse health consequences or death to humans or animals."

Food and Drug Administration Safety and Innovation Act of 2012 (FDASIA)

FDASIA[51] reauthorizes and amends the existing user fee statute for drugs, the Prescription Drug User Fee Act (PDUFA), and establishes two new laws, the Generic Drug User Fee Act (GDUFA) and the Biosimilar User Fee Act (BsUFA), that set out fee structures for generic drugs and biosimilars, respectively. FDASIA also empowers FDA to require electronic submission of drug information for importers as a condition of granting entry of their products into the United States and requires FDA (once the agency has specified a unique facility identifier system) to ensure that its databases are adequate to facilitate risk-based inspections. This broadened emphasis on more effective inspection imposes more robust record-keeping requirements on manufacturers, requiring that establishments provide (in either electronic or physical form), in advance or instead of inspection, records that FDA has requested. Failure to submit the proper records or pay facility fees under GDUFA can result in all products at the relevant facility (including both drugs and APIs manufactured in the

---

[51] (Commissioner, 2016b)

facility or containing an ingredient manufactured in such facility) being deemed misbranded.

Food Safety Modernization Act (FSMA)[52]

The burden is on food processors to maintain extensive supporting documentation that identifies their potential hazards and confirms adequate preventive controls of those hazards. As a result, food companies are focused on developing appropriate internal policies and procedures as well as necessary to address compliance challenges. FDA is required to designate high-risk foods for which additional recordkeeping requirements are adequate and appropriate and to establish recordkeeping requirements for these foods. High-risk foods requirements are designed to identify high-risk foods so that they can be rapidly identified, effectively tracked, and traced during a foodborne illness outbreak or another event.

Current Good Manufacturing Practices (cCGMPs)[53]

GMP recordkeeping requirements mandate development and maintenance of detailed records. FDA uses those records to determine whether the methods, facilities, and controls used in manufacturing, processing, packing and holding of drugs conform to current good manufacturing practices. A finished drug, which does not comply with these requirements, is adulterated. A manufacturer of an adulterated drug is subject to potentially severe sanctions including product seizure and criminal penalties. Violations of provisions requiring that labels

---

[52] (Center, Safety, and Nutrition, 2017)
[53] (Center, Safety, and Nutrition, 2015)

declare the identity of the manufacturer (unless the omissions were part of a plan to avoid detection) may be evaluated "low." The seriousness of GMP violations will vary. Thus, a violation of a recordkeeping requirement might be "low," whereas a failure to ensure the effectiveness of the product would probably be "high." The purpose of these Recordkeeping requirements is to enable a manufacturer and FDA to identify and investigate any problems that may arise with a drug product. Failure to have these records available for an investigation could prevent resolution of undesirable conditions that can seriously compromise public health.

Biologics, Blood and Vaccine Regulations[54]

Inspection of Human Cells, Tissues, and Cellular and Tissue-Based Products (HCT/Ps), For Vaccines, and Blood & Biologics. The inspection of human cells, tissues, and cellular and tissue-based products (HCT/Ps), for vaccines, blood and Biologics raise concerns that disease transmission could occur. These concerns coupled with information derived from these investigations prompted the FDA to publish an interim rule in December 1993 that specifically required certain communicable disease testing, donor screening, and record-keeping for human tissue intended for transplantation. On November 18, 2004, FDA issued regulations that require establishments that manufacture HCT/Ps to comply with Current Good Tissue Practices (CGTP), which would include, among other things, proper handling, processing, labeling, and record-keeping procedures. The regulations

[54] (Center and Evaluation, 2015)

require each establishment to maintain a quality program to ensure compliance with CGTP. The firm must periodically perform a quality audit, for management review. Computers: The performance of computer software must be validated (if customized) or verified (if used "off-the-shelf") for the intended purpose if the firm relies upon it to comply with core CGTP requirements. If the company is using a computerized record-keeping/ tracking system, ensure the integrity of records is maintained and traceability of all HCT/Ps from donor to the consignee or final disposition; and from the consignee or final disposition to the donor.

Medical Device and Diagnostics Regulations (MDR)[55]

If you are a user facility, importer, or manufacturer, you must establish and maintain MDR (Medical Device Reporting) event files. You must clearly identify all MDR event files and maintain them to facilitate timely access. Your MDR event files must contain information in your possession or references to information related to the adverse event, copies of all MDR forms and other information related to the event. You must permit any authorized FDA employee, at all reasonable times, to access, to copy, and to verify the records required by this part. If you are a user facility, you must retain an MDR event file relating to an adverse event for a period of 2 years from the date of the event. If you are a device distributor, you must establish and maintain device complaint records (files). Your records must contain any incident information, including any written, electronic, or oral

[55] (Center and Health, 2016)

communication, either received or generated by you, that alleges deficiencies related to the identity (e.g., labeling), quality, durability, reliability, safety, effectiveness, or performance of a device. You must also maintain information about your evaluation of the allegations, if any, in the incident record. You must clearly identify the records as device incident records and file these records by device name. You may maintain these records in written or electronic format. You must back up any file maintained in electronic format.

You must retain copies of the required device incident records for two years from the date of inclusion of the record in the file or for a period equivalent to the expected life of the device, whichever is greater. You must maintain copies of these records for this period even if you no longer distribute the device. You must maintain the device complaint files established under this section at your principal business establishment. If you are also a manufacturer, you may maintain the file at the same location as you maintain your complaint file under part 820 of this chapter. You must permit any authorized FDA employee, at all reasonable times, to access, to copy, and to verify the records required by this part.

Drug Quality and Security Act (DQSA)[56]

The Drug Quality and Security Act (DQSA) was signed into law on November 28th 2013. This bill has two titles:

- Title I – Drug Compounding
- Title II – Drug Supply Chain Security Act (DSCSA)

---

[56] (PLAW 113publ54, 2013)

The DSCSA is intended to improve patient safety by establishing a national standard for drug supply chain security. The Federal Bill will deactivate the recent California e-Pedigree law and the patchwork of approximately 30 other state drug pedigree laws. The DSCSA will establish one national standard for track and trace requirements for drug distribution and will allow GSK to take a standardized approach to providing compliance data to trading partners

The DSCSA requires the following:

Jan 1st 2015 – Prior to or at the time of each transaction in which there is a transfer of ownership of a product, a manufacturer is required to provide the subsequent owner with lot level transaction information (TI), transaction history (TH) and transaction statement (TS). This information needs to be in a single document, paper or electronic format is acceptable for the first 4 years. After year 4 the information is required to be in electronic format only

Jan 1st 2015 – A wholesale distributor that does not physically handle or store product shall be exempt from these provisions provided the manufacturer that distributes the product to the dispenser by the means of a drop shipment for such wholesale distributor includes on the TI, TH to the dispenser the contact information for such wholesale distributor and provides the TI, TH, and TS directly to the dispenser

Jan 1st 2015 – A manufacturer is required to capture the TI, TH and TS for each transaction and maintain for not less than 6 years after the date of the transaction

Jan 1st 2015 – The trading partners of a manufacturer will only be authorized trading partners. An authorized Trading Partners is defined as having a valid license under state law

Jan 1st 2015 - Upon a request by the Secretary (FDA) or other appropriate Federal or State official, in the event of a recall or for the purpose of investigating suspect product or illegitimate product, manufacturers are required to support the ability to validate any applicable product transaction information and transaction history in response to such investigations. Applicable transaction information must be provided within 1 business day, not to exceed 48 hours, after receiving the request

Nov 28th 2017 – Manufacturers are required to encode all drug products with a unique product identifier at smallest saleable unit and sealed homogenous case. Manufacturers will maintain the product identifier information for not less than 6 years after the date of the transaction

4 Years after enactment – Manufacturers are required to support requests for verification at the unit level (serial #) not later than 24 hours after receiving the request

4 Years after enactment – Upon receipt of a returned product that the manufacturer intends to further distribute, before further distributing such product, the manufacturer will shall verify the

product identifier including the serial # for each homogenous case or saleable unit

Data Quality Legislation

Regulatory agencies expect that data be reliable and accurate. CGMP regulations and FDA guidance documents allow flexible and risk-based strategies to prevent and detect data integrity issues. Firms should implement meaningful and effective risk-based strategies to manage their data integrity risks. Decisions on how to implement the system must be based upon their process understanding and knowledge management of technologies and business models. Agencies want to make sure that the conditions under which information is processed ensure data, authenticity, reliability, legibility, and integrity.

Uniform Photographic Copies of Business & Public Records as Evidence Act 28 U.S. Code § 1732[57]

If any business, institution, member of a profession, or any department or agency of government, in the regular course of business or activity has kept or recorded any memorandum, writing, entry, print, representation or combination thereof, of any act, transaction, occurrence, or event, and in the regular course of business has caused any or all of the same to be recorded, copied, or reproduced by any photographic, photostatic, microfilm, micro-card, miniature photographic, or other process which accurately reproduces or forms a durable medium for so reproducing the original, the original may be

---

[57] (USCODE 2011 title28 partV chap115 sec1732, 2012)

destroyed in the regular course of business unless its preservation is required by law. Such reproduction, when satisfactorily identified, is as admissible in evidence as the original itself in any judicial or administrative proceeding whether the original is in existence or not and an enlargement or facsimile of such reproduction is likewise admissible in evidence if the original reproduction is in existence and available for inspection under direction of the court.

21 CFR Part 11

Provides guidance on establishing security measures for Electronic Records And Signatures. FDA suggest that your decision to validate computerized systems must take into account the impact the systems have on your ability to meet predicate rule requirements. Your firm should seriously consider the impact those systems might have on the accuracy, reliability, integrity, availability, and authenticity of required records and signatures. Even if there is no predicate rule requirement to validate a system, in some instances it may still be important to validate the system. We recommend that you based your approach on a justified and documented risk assessment and a determination of the potential of the system to affect product quality and safety and record integrity.

Uniform Electronic Transactions Act (UETA)[58]

A law individually adopted by 47 states, the District of Columbia, Puerto Rico, and the US Virginia Islands Both ESIGN and UETA establish that electronic records and signatures carry the same

[58] (Brumfield et al., 2000)

weight and legal effect as traditional paper documents and handwritten signatures, stating. The definition in this Act is broad and is used to illustrate one way of establishing attribution or content integrity of an electronic record or signature. The use of a security procedure is not accorded operative legal effect, through the use of presumptions or otherwise, by this Act. In this Act, the use of security procedures is simply one method for proving the source or content of an electronic record or signature.

Application Integrity Policy (AIP)[59]

FDA invokes the AIP when a company's actions raise significant questions about the integrity of data in drug applications. In this case, the FDA stops all substantive scientific review of new or pending drug approval applications that contain data generated by the facility in question. The basic logic is that if an applicant engages in practices that raise significant doubts about the reliability of data used to support one or more applications, FDA must pause to assess whether the data in any of the applicant's submissions are reliable.

Electronic Signatures in Global and National Commerce Act (ESIGN or E-SIGN)[60]

E-SIGN Act implements a national uniform standard for all electronic transactions that encourages the use of electronic signatures, electronic contracts, and electronic records by providing legal certainty for these instruments when signatories comply with its

---

[59] (Karen.Stutsman, 2004)

[60] (ELECTRONIC SIGNATURES IN GLOBAL AND NATIONAL COMMERCE ACT, 1910)

standards. The E-SIGN Act includes several key provisions that address: consumer consent requirements, validity requirements for electronic signatures, electronic contracts and electronic records, retention requirements for electronic contracts and records, E-SIGN seeks to assure accuracy, record integrity, and accessibility of records that are required to be retained.

Federal Rules of Civil Procedure (FRCP)[61]

The primary objective of the initial disclosure obligation is to accelerate the exchange of electronic communications and data compilations used in court cases and to eliminate the paperwork involved in requesting such information. These rules govern the procedure in all civil actions and proceedings in the United States district courts. They should be construed, administered, and employed by the court and the parties to secure the just, speedy, and inexpensive determination of every action and proceeding. It is anticipated that Judicial Conference standards will govern such technical specifications as data formatting, the speed of transmission means to transmit copies of supporting documents, and security of communication. Perhaps more important, standards must be established to assure proper maintenance and integrity of the record and to provide appropriate access and retrieval mechanisms.

Privacy and Data Protection

The Privacy Act prohibits the disclosure of a record about an individual from a system of records absent the written consent of the

---

[61] (Ltd, 2016)

individual unless the disclosure is under one of twelve statutory exceptions. The Act also provides individuals with a means by which to seek access to an amendment of their records and sets forth various agency record-keeping requirements. Regulatory agencies want to make sure that the conditions under which information is processed ensure data confidentiality, privacy, security, data availability

NARA Technical Guidelines for Digitizing Archival Materials for Electronic Access[62]

NARA Technical Guidelines are intended to be informative, and not intended to be prescriptive. However, records management metadata should still include documentation on access and usage restrictions - even unrestricted records should be identified as "unrestricted." This may be important metadata to express at the system level as well, as controls over access to and use of digital resources might be built directly into a delivery or access system. It develops communication around Metadata element sets for intellectual property and rights for defining reproduction and distribution policies. At a minimum, rights-related metadata should include: the legal status of the record; a statement on who owns the physical and intellectual aspects of the record; contact information for these rights holders; as well as any restrictions associated with the copying, use, and distribution of the record. To facilitate bringing digital copies into future repositories, it is desirable to collect appropriate rights management metadata at the time of creation of the digital copies. At the very least, digital versions should be identified

[62] (Puglia et al., 2014)

with a designation of copyright status, such as: "public domain;" "copyrighted" (and whether clearance/permissions from rights holder has been secured); "unknown;" and "donor agreement/contract..

Uniform Commercial Code (UCC)[63]

First published in 1952, is one of some uniform acts that have been promulgated with the goal of harmonizing the law of sales and other commercial transactions across the United States of America (U.S.). Provides guidance and advice on a standardized record retention schedule, conducting an annual file-cleanup to dispose of unnecessary documents. It sets forth minimum retention periods for receipts and other related records

Uniform Preservation of Private Business Records Act (UPPBRA)[64]

UPPBRA defines records as "books of account, vouchers, documents, canceled checks, payrolls, correspondence, records of sales, personnel, equipment and production, reports relating to any or all of such records, and other business papers." UPPBRA allows for (but does not require) destruction of these documents three years from the date they are produced. Associations and member companies are also subject to criminal penalties under provisions of the Sarbanes-Oxley Act of 2002, passed in connection with the securities fraud scandals of recent years, and which prohibits corruptly tampering,

---

[63] (STATUTE 77 Pg630, no date)

[64] (805 ILCS 410/ uniform preservation of private business records act, 2003)

altering, destroying or concealing records to prevent their availability for use in an "official proceeding."

Sarbanes-Oxley Act (Sox)[65]

Requires that CEOs and CFOs be held accountable for the content of financial statements. Sox regulate the type and length of time of accounting records are stored and the types of controls that must be in place over financial data.

The Health Insurance Portability and Accountability Act (HIPAA)[66]

HIPPA establishes nationwide standards for health information. Individuals, organizations, and agencies that meet the definition of a covered entity must protect the privacy and security of health information and must provide individuals with certain rights on their health information..

Safe Harbor

Safe Harbor is the name of a policy agreement established between the United States Department of Commerce and the European Union (E.U.) in November 2000. It is designed to regulate the way that U.S. companies export and handle personal data. Safe Harbor stipulations require that companies collecting personal data must inform people that the data is being gathered, and tell them what will be done with it. They must also obtain permission to pass on the information to a third party.

---

[65] (Sarbanes-Oxley act of 2002, 2004)
[66] (Summary of the HIPAA privacy rule, 2013)

To bridge these differences and provide a streamlined and cost-effective means for U.S. organizations to satisfy the directive's "adequacy" requirement, the U.S. Department of Commerce in consultation with the European Commission developed a "safe harbor" framework. The U.S./EU safe harbor framework is an important way for U.S. organizations to avoid experiencing interruptions in their business dealings with the EU or facing prosecution by EU member state authorities under EU member state privacy laws. Self-certifying to the U.S.-EU the Safe Harbor framework will ensure that EU organizations know that a company is provided with "adequate" privacy protection, as defined by the directive.

Health Insurance Portability and Accountability Act (HIPPA)

HIPPA, developed by the Department of Health and Human Services, provides patients with access to their medical records, giving them more control over how their personal health information is used and disclosed. It is a U.S. law designed to provide privacy standards that protect patients' medical records and other health information that are issued to health plans, doctors, hospitals and other health care providers along with matters that relate to health plans.

FISMA – The Federal Information Security Management Act (FISMA)

FISMA[67] strengthens Federal Government information security, including through the requirement for the development of mandatory information security risk management standards. Information Security Management Act FISMA provides development of the major security standards and guidelines to support the implementation of and compliance with the Federal Government. Their vision is to promote the development of critical standards for categorizing information systems and develop minimum-security requirements and security controls for information systems.

GLBA – The Gramm-Leach-Bliley Act of 1999 (GLBA)

GLBA[68] is a set of rules designed to controls the use of consumers' private information. Identified Organizations must provide technical, administrative, and physical safeguards to protect the customer's information from unauthorized disclosure, alteration, or deletion. Some rules prohibit the sharing of certain kinds of customers' personal financial information with unaffiliated parties. Organizations must take reasonable steps to business with services providers that are capable of safeguarding the protected customer information.

18 U.S. Code Chapter 121 - Stored Wire And Electronic Communications And Transactional Records Access[69]

This code is designed to protect the privacy of stored electronic communications. This includes storage before transmission to a recipient as well as any copy of the transmitted communications kept after delivery to a recipient. A person or entity that provides a public

---

[67] (FISMA final, no date)
[68] (PLAW 106publ102, 1914)
[69] (United States code, 2010 edition title 18 -CRIMES AND CRIMINAL PROCEDURE PART I -CRIMES CHAPTER 121 -STORED WIRE AND ELECTRONIC COMMUNICATIONS AND TRANSACTIONAL RECORDS ACCESS, 2010)

electronic communication service, or remote computing service, shall not knowingly divulge the contents of a communication held in electronic storage by the individual or company. The same holds true about any communication carried on or maintained by, any public remote computing service. Included in the preceding are communications received by way of electronic transmission, created using computer processing, or held solely for storage or computer processing.

Chapter 5

Standards

"He's the guy that came up with Sigma One."

In addition to adhering to GXPs, companies must consider adopting additional standard-setting activities. These other activities set baseline expectations for the performance of computer systems, utilities, facilities, devices, instruments, laboratory systems, and more. Senior management within these companies must develop a framework of policies, procedures, methodologies, practices, standards, protocols, criteria and specifications for determining how it will function. Standards must be leveraged at every level within the organization. Regulated industries rely on the use of standards that are developed by external standards organizations on a daily basis. These standards provide industry-accepted methodologies not captured in the GXPs. Standards can be rules, guidelines, procedures, specifications designs, measurements, test methods, sampling procedures, conditions, common practices, and even descriptions of objects physical dimensions. Standards can be used to describe specific patterns of behavior such as the way a person approaches a matter, a specific way of doing something or process, practice, a technique that is used or a methodical operation or systematic operation. Finding appropriate flexible standards that fit in with the company's processes is a soul searching process. Some standards are very complex and may be precarious to apply, while others are widely accepted throughout the industry. Finding the right standards for governing certain behaviors within your organization can be very challenging.

Healthcare companies may understand the importance of developing unique specifications for bottles used in the packaging drug products, but they do not necessarily manufacture the bottles used in the packaging process. The bottle manufacturer is supposedly the expert in understanding the container's composition, dispensing technologies, stability profile, impact and chemical resistance, tensile strength, color, and the different plastics used to make the endless shapes. The bottle manufacturer is an expert in developing an array of materials with an unlimited amount of profiles. Healthcare companies core competency is specialized in developing and administering drug products that are safe. They rely on the bottle manufacturer to provide bottles that are safe to use. The bottle manufacturer must provide containers that adhere to specific standards that will be able to handle the rigors shipping, storage, shelf life, seasonal variations, and more. Regulatory agencies encourage companies who handle regulated products to reach out to standards organizations for guidance in establishing well-defined practices. Regulatory agencies realize that if there were no standard organizations, then each company would have to develop a unique process for doing the same industry related task. Just imagine if every company who submitted a drug application have a unique process assuring that computer system used in the industry are functioning as expected.

Regulatory agencies would have hundreds of thousands of different methodologies to review. However, if a handful of standard organizations could publish a few standards for 80 percent of submissions, it would reduce the time needed by agencies to assess and verify the science. Regulatory and government agencies have limited resources. They are not in the business of developing industry standards. Regulatory agencies know some of the challenges the healthcare companies face. That is why they are proactive in fostering cooperation among the standard organizations and healthcare manufacturers. Regulatory agencies provide guidance and the legal framework; pharmaceutical companies provide safe products that meet the public's needs, and standards organizations develop everything that's not being addressed by the government and industry. In some cases, Regulatory agencies will create incentives for standards organizations to guide an industry. Government regulations form a global network that is designed to protect its citizens. If you collaborate with them, your products and services stand a greater chance of being adopted globally. A regulatory endorsement in a journal or references in guidance documentation could make or break your endeavors.

Regulatory agencies promote the use of good standards via the development of regulation and policy. In many cases, agencies adopt standards from non-government organizations and inter-governmental international standards organizations. These organizations' standards are adopted and referenced by regulatory agencies. If some portion of the standard is in conflict with the regulatory agencies approach, the Regulatory agency will partially adopt the portion of the standard that best represents its regulatory policy. Just because regulatory agencies decide to adopt a set of standards from a non-governmental organization, does not mean that it completely endorses all of the standards that are being promoted from that organization. Nor does it suggest that the agency is committed to supporting the efforts of that organization. Standard recognition is not mandatory. If you do not follow a particular non-governmental standard, it does not mean that you are breaking the law.

Regulatory agency always has the option to augment voluntary consensus standards by adding recommendations in the guidance publications. Likewise, the agencies commitment to standards can be withdrawn at any time. Standards are simply tools that can be used by an organization to help align with its goals and agency policy. There are many standards that are referenced by regulatory agencies that can be used in industry to support their processes. The FDA prefers to use standards that are internationally harmonized. Agencies will purposely involve representatives from diversified countries to collaborate on standard usage. International standards are adopted as long as those standards are pinpointed for a particular purpose and do not conflict with the U.S. agenda.

Voluntary Consensus Standards

Voluntary Consensus Standards are standards that are developed by voluntary consensus standard bodies, (industry associations and professionals) for voluntary use. These organizations have agreed to make their standards available free of charge. There are no royalties or costs are associated with using the use of their standards. They have agreed to make their intellectual property available domestically or internationally in some cases to develop a consensus on the use of the standard. In order to develop a consensus on the use of their proprietary procedure, the owners of the intellectual properties have agreed to make their intellectual property available for use by the public. The public can comment and readily use the standard. The standards organization gets to determine if the standard needs tweaking are scraping.

Regulatory agencies encourage the use of Voluntary Consensus Standards. Voluntary Consensus Standards are standards that are derived from industry consensus. Generally, There is no question about their validity because they are commonly used. Some Voluntary Consensus Standards are generally recognized as safe because industry and governments around the world are currently using them. Therefore, adoption of the standards does not require extensive testing.

Some standards are owned by their authors and they are protected by international copyright laws. These standards are considered intellectual property and is copyright protected by the United States government and international laws. They cannot be used without compensating the owner for using it. Permission and/or compensation must be acquired in order for them to be utilized. Standards are intellectual property of its authors. In most cases, it is ok to cite the use of Voluntary Consensus Standards.

Performance Standards

Most performance standards are based upon specific performance specifications. Performance specifications provide indicators (Availability, Response time, Transmission time, Processing speed, Channel capacity, Latency, Bandwidth, Throughput, Relative efficiency, Scalability, Bandwidth, Throughput and Scalability) for what was performed or what must be established. For example, when testing the functionality of a computerized systems one indicator of performance could be speed. An indication of how computerized systems performing is GHz. Questions regarding the systems performance could be; how fast is the system? Does it initialize quickly? Service providers have specific performance expectations or standard performance metrics (CPU, RAM, hard drive, backup, display, network performance, etc.). So a standard that can be used universally to determine how computers perfom can be extremely valuable.

Non-government Standards

Non-government standards are standards that's developed within the private sector. The word private sector could mean community or citizen-based organization, business association, social organization or an organizations that has an agenda. Widely accepted standards are developed on a collaborative, consensus basis. These standards could have been tested at universities, manufacturing plants, testing laboratories and more. In some cases where and organization develops a standard that makes good scientific sense, these organizations receive may help from the regulatory agencies promoting the standard. Standards organizations are in the business of planning, developing, establishing and coordinating, specifications, and guidelines.

The pharmaceutical industry uses hundreds of standards. Most non-governmental standard organizations allow user to purchase a licenses to use and provide tech support the standard as long as their standard is being used as intended. Many standards organizations try to align their science with the needs of regulatory agencies. It is a good thing when a standard is recognized in a regulatory journal. The recognition is like finding gold in a river. This endorsement helps to make the standard more palatable.

Standards organizations consist of but isnt limited to Voluntary Standards Consensus organizations, the Non-Governmental Standard Organizations, as well as the Performance Standards Organizations. This below listining is not exhaustive but includes technical expertise from recognized consensus standards from the following highly regarded organizations: AIUM, ANSI, ASA, ASME, ASTM, CEN, CGA, CLSI, NCCLS, IEC IEEE, ISO, NEMA. NFPA, RESNA, IESNA, UL, USP, AOAC, etc.. No one standard can define all of the activities needed to produce safe products and or speak to all industry activities. Nevertheless, public and private standard organizations provide a great service to the pharmaceutical industry. These groups provide a scientific methodology for developing meaningful products and services. Most of these organizations have their own specific expertise. There area of focus is their claim to fame. The expertise within the standard groups can vary. At the end of the day, It is the methodology (policies, procedures, methodologies, practices, standards, protocols, criteria and specifications) used by the organizations that is aligned with the FDA's objectives, standards, acts and policies.

Standards organizations provide a myriad guidance and codes that are recognized by regulated industries for support good practices. The FDA promotes these standards organizations because their methodology aligns with FDA objectives, standards, laws, and policies. In addition to FDA referenced standards they are hundreds of additional standards used by regulated industries that support good practices. Many of the standards are not adopted by the FDA as mission-critical but have been recognized as major contributors to good practices. Many standards organizations such as, NAS, GAMP, ISPE, NIST, SOX, HiPPA, may not be critical or central to FDA's long-term goals, but they are recognized as major contributors to good practices.

Be familiar with the standards

Why is it important to become familiar the different standards? It is important to become familiar with the policies, procedures, methodologies, practices, standards, protocols, criteria and specifications, and common practices used in regulated spaces because you might host information created by use of these standards. For example, if a Healthcare company adopted a global process for validating Computerized Systems then you need to know what standard is being used. If a companywide standard exist for validating computerized systems has been submitted to regulatory agencies, you need to make sure you are following it. Every time you make changes to your environment, the change process should mimic what standards are being followed upstream and downstream to your process.

Suppose you are providing managed support for incidents, problems, events or task, emergency or routine, operating system, control panel, server setup and any pre-installed applications that are managed with automated backup and monitoring. It is great that you have your own practices in place for these activities. However, you must overlook existing processes that have been implemented at the client's site. Do not assume that all standards are equal. Your process for handling incident management may not have the same rigors at the client site. Every time you make changes to the virtual environment, you should ensure that you are aligned with the clients regulatory wishes. The last thing you need is to be in a multitenant environment and have regulatory agencies audit your systems for lack of compliance.

Regulated businesses are not built in a vacuum. They have many contributors. In addition to understanding your role in the information management process its good to know how processes relating to computerized systems are derived. The following standards organizations make considerable contributions to the regulated space. Some of them may not directly affect how you conduct business but should be considered when managing information in the regulated space.

---

[70] (AIUM, 2017)

American Institute of Ultrasound in Medicine (AIUM)[70]

AIUM has established a series of practices for the medical ultrasound community. These practices contain the minimum guidelines for the use of ultrasound technology. AIUM practices are accepted and referenced by regulatory agencies. AIUM has developed policies, practice standards, safety procedures, and performance guidelines for ultrasound professionals. The professionals applying these procedures are physicians, sonographers, scientists, engineers, other healthcare providers, and manufacturers of ultrasound equipment. AIUM sets the standards for acoustic output measurement in diagnostic ultrasound equipment, real-time display of thermal and medical acoustic output indices on diagnostic ultrasound equipment, and acoustic output labeling for diagnostic ultrasound equipment.

American National Standards Institute (ANSI)[71]

Established in October 1918, ANSI, a nonprofit organization, ensures the health, safety, and welfare of the American public. They oversee the development and its implementation, along with the assessment of guidelines, criteria, and standards and how its use will affect the United States. ANSI is the official representative of the

---

[71] (ANSI-American national standards institute, 2017)

United States government to the International Organization for Standardization (ISO) and overseas the United States voluntary standardization process. Because of the FDA Modernization Act of 1997, ANSI has been given authority to identify a standards development process by which standards can receive recognition in an open and transparent process. Computer standards from ANSI include the American Standard Code for Information Interchange (ASCII) and the Small Computer System Interface (SCSI). ANSI also sponsored standard Joint Technical Committee ISO/IEC 27018. ISO/IEC 27018 defines Information technology Security techniques for protection of personally identifiable information (PII) in public clouds acting as PII processors. ISO/IEC 27018 establishes a uniform, international approach to protecting PII stored in the cloud.

Acoustical Society of America (ASA)[72]

ASA has helped to define what a hearing aid is, how it is to be used, and its classification. By working with the FDA, ASA has determined what is expected from hearing aid technology. ASA has developed three import standards:

1. American National Standard For Rating Noise on Speech Interference
2. American National Standard Criteria for Evaluating Room Noise
3. American National Standard Testing Hearing Aids - Part 2: Methods for characterizing signal processing in

[72] (2815, Thursday, Bureau, Register, tab, et al., 2017a)

hearing aids with a speech-like signal (a nationally adopted international standard) American National Standard For Rating Noise on Speech Interference

ASAP's mission is to foster understanding of the role that technology plays in assisting pharmacists to promote patient safety and the proper use of medications, comply with laws and regulations, and operate their practices more efficiently by providing a forum for sharing diverse knowledge and perspectives on the modern practice of pharmacy.

American Society of Mechanical Engineers (ASME)[73]

ASME provides technical expertise to engineers from the United States, Belgium, India, and China and throughout the world codes and standards that will ensure the safety of the mechanical process. ASME has over 500 codes and standards. Two familiar standards are:

- Safety Standard for Pressure Vessels for Human Occupancy

ASME contains design and functional requirements for piping typically found in petroleum refineries; chemical, pharmaceutical, textile, paper, semiconductor, and cryogenic plants; and related processing plants and terminals. It covers materials and components, design, fabrication, assembly, erection, examination, inspection, and testing of piping.

American Society for Testing and Materials International (ASTM) [74]

ASTM is an international standards organization that develops and publishes voluntary consensus technical standards for a wide range of

[73] (The American society of mechanical engineers, 2017)
[74] (ASTM, 1996)

materials, products, systems, and services. The organization's headquarters is in West Conshohocken, Pennsylvania, about five miles. (8.0 km) Northwest of Philadelphia. Representing the American Section of the International Association for Testing, ASTM was founded in 1898. It has a dominant role among standards developers in the USA, and it claims to be the worlds largest developer of standards. Using a consensus process, ASTM supports thousands of volunteer technical committees. Drawing its members from around the world, it collectively develops and maintains more than 12,000 standards. ASTM International, known until 2001 as the American Society for Testing and MaterialsASTM "Standard E 2500 was approved in the second quarter of 2007. It describes a risk-based and science-based approach to the specification, design, and verification of manufacturing systems and equipment. The FDA has publicly supported the ASTM standard setting process.

European Committee for Standardization (CEN)[75]

CEN is established under Belgian law. It is a nonprofit organization that was founded in 1975 for the purpose of developing voluntary European standards. Representing 33 countries in Europe, their standards are national. Their goal is to be a central standards organization that goods and services can be marketed to its members. CEN has over

[75] (Home, 2017)

60,000 subject matter experts in various industries and has the potential of influencing the lives of over 600 million people.

Compressed Gas Association (CGA)[76]

CGA, founded in 1913, specializes in many different aspects of the compressed gas industry promoting its development of safety standards. Its involvement in the medical gas industry is important to the FDA. Also, it distributes technical specifications and training material around the world. Because of the CGA manufactures, transports, stores, trance fills, disposes of many different forms of gaseous waste, it is involved in technical specifications. The technical specifications include but are not limited to protection and safety, advocacy and leadership, involvement in the design, and providing standards.

Clinical and Laboratory Standards Institute (CLSI)[77]

CLSI has been developing clinical laboratory testing standards for over 40 years. Their focus is to provide quality testing standards for the global laboratory community. CLSI believes in a consensus-driven process in which a community of laboratories, government agencies, and healthcare professionals drive the standardization within the laboratory industry. When ideas are put into a community environment, the outcome would only be excellence, and superior

[76] (cganet)
[77] (Clinical and Institute, no date)

quality of service CLSI relies on its global partners for producing standards that are relevant for today's laboratory industry and that elevates the quality of products and services worldwide.

International Electrotechnical Commission (IEC)[78]

IEC standards are used in developing standards for the electronics and power industry. Established in 1906, IEC has developed into the world's largest international standards organization. It specializes in developing standards for electronics, power and electronics related industries and is a consensus-based organization: an organization which every member is considered a stakeholder. Over 10,000 subject matter experts from various industries participate in the IEC standardization process. Electrotechnical interests of governments, regulatory agencies, educational institutions and the business community can be traced back to standardization development and IEC.

1. Medical Electrical Equipment is Particular requirements for the safety of lung ventilators - Critical care ventilators
2. Medical Electrical Equipment is Particular requirements for the safety and essential performance of anesthetic systems.
3. Medical Electrical Equipment is Particular requirements for the basic safety and essential

[78] (Welcome to the IEC - international Electrotechnical commission, 2016)

performance of transcutaneous partial pressure monitoring equipment.

4. Medical Electrical Equipment is Particular requirements for the safety and essential performance of anesthetic systems.
5. Medical Electrical Equipment is Particular requirements for the basic safety and essential performance of automated noninvasive sphygmomanometers.

Institute of Electrical and Electronics Engineers (IEEE)[79]

IEEE, was founded in 1948 and is one of the largest professional organizations in the world. Its focus is on advancing technology. IEEE produces brochures, technical journals, educational events, conferences, seminars, publications are focused on the advancement of technology for the benefit of humanity and improving global conditions. IEEE has close to 400,000 members and over one hundred 160 countries and is responsible for over 900 active standards. It is the world's largest technical/professional organization.

6. American National Standard Methods of Measurement of Compatibility between Wireless Communication Devices and Hearing Aids
7. Calibration and Usage of "Dose Calibrator" Ionization Chambers for the Assay of Radionuclides
8. Health informatics - Point-of-care medical devices communication - Part 10101: Nomenclature
9. Health informatics - Personal health device communication - Part 10417: Device specialization - Glucose meter

---

[79] (IEEE, 2017)

10. Calibration and Usage of "Dose Calibrator" Ionization Chambers for the Assay of Radionuclides

International Organization for Standardization (ISO)[80]

Since 1947, ISO has been in the business of providing voluntary international standards. This is important because it represents the input of scientists around the world. Its goal is to provide state-of-the-art standards that can be used in products and services around the world for the purpose of making people's lives more efficient and productive. Its standards are being used in industries such as healthcare food safety, computers, and agriculture. The standards are voluntary and are developed in a global consensus environment. This collaborative environment allows governments, return bodies businesses, and everyday people to have ~~it~~ an equal playing field.

The National Electrical Manufacturers Association (NEMA)[81]

NEMA, founded in 1926, is an association of manufacturers who specialize in electrical equipment and medical imaging. Their goal is to increase market shares by increasing the distribution network. NEMA believes that if they promote innovation and safety, they can enhance their products and services within the electrical medical imaging community. Most of NEMA constituents are from and focus on North American and its manufacturing community. FEMA has over 400 members with a market capitalization of over $140 billion.

---

[80] (copyright, 2017)
[81] (NEMA, 2016)
[82] (NFPA, 2016)

National Fire Protection Association (NFPA)[82]

Established in 1896, this association's goal was to reduce and restrain fires. Since then NFPA has developed over 300 consensus codes and standards. It leads the world in training and educating people about fire codes. NFPA focuses on reducing the risk of fire by establishing criteria for buildings and design. With over 6000 volunteers, the association also proposes and revises terms standards. NFPA codes and standards are distributed free of charge.

Rehabilitation Engineering and Assistive Technology Society (RESNA)[83]

RESNA's goal is to use technology for the improvement of lifestyles regarding people with disabilities. They provide certification and continuing education to those individuals who have the same goals. RESNA sponsors forums for encouraging collaboration on rehabilitation technology. RESNA has developed technology standards for meeting the needs of people with disabilities.

Illuminating Engineering Society of North America (IES)[84]

IES was founded in 1906, communicates information about good lighting practices in the forms of publications, services, programs, and

[83] (RESNA, 2016)
[84] (superuser, 2010)

events. This organization is the central technical hub for good lighting practices. IES is responsible for publishing over 100 professional publications that include illuminations for architects, governments, engineers, distributors, designers, research institutions for sports, recreational, streets, museums, stadiums, schools, and more. IES has well over 1000 members distributed among North and South America as well as the world. Its committees have responsibility for developing standards for use in energy management, testing, measuring, and other phenomena.

Underwriters Laboratories (UL)[85]

Having been in business for over 100 years, UL has five vibrant vertical markets that it does business in verification services, space product safety, environment, space life and health, and knowledge services. UL's mission is in promoting product safety testing and certification. However, its expertise includes certifying, validating, auditing, advising, testing, and training the public. The focus is to ensure product safety for the consumer by simplifying compliance and regulatory issues, and it hopes to increase global trade and market growth. In addition to addressing global business needs, UL has created a series of standards for assessing systems and performance, test components, and products such as food and water, environmental, renewable energies, recycling, and other technologies. UL has well over 1000 standards.

---

[85] (UL, 2017)

U.S. Pharmacopeia Convention (USP)[86]

The USP, a nonprofit organization, began its operation in 1820. It includes a group of physicians that work on developing a national lexicon of drug names and formulas for the United States. The USP provides quality, ID, strength, efficacy, and purity of food ingredients, dietary supplements, and medicines for the world. Currently, the organization provides reference standards that are recognized as official industry standards. It is involved in the creation of documentary standards (USP–NF Is this a documentary standard or notation?), dietary supplement compendiums, and food chemicals codices whose materials are based upon official monographs that are enforceable by the US government.

Association of Analytical Communities (AOAC)[87]

AOAC, founded in 1884, is a nonprofit voluntary consensus standards organization. Universities, government agencies, research institutions, international organizations, technology and instrument leaders, and contract research organizations are the building blocks of this organization. AOAC develops voluntary standards for global use. With over 3000 members spanning over four continents, AOAC represents the efforts of a vast volunteer organization.

---

[86] (USP, 2017)
[87] (International, 2016)
[88] (Sciences, 2016)

National Academy of Sciences/National Research Council[88]

NATIONAL ACADEMY OF SCIENCES

In 1966 the FDA contracted with the National Academy of Sciences/National Research Council to measure the effectiveness of 4,000 marketed drugs approved by safety alone between 1938 and 1962. The National Academy of Sciences (NAS) is a private, non-profit society of distinguished scholars. Established by an Act of Congress, signed by President Abraham Lincoln in 1863, the NAS is entrusted with providing independent, objective advice to the nation on matters related to science and technology. Scientists are elected by their peers for membership into the NAS because of outstanding contributions in research The National Academy of Sciences/The National Research Council, and the Drug Efficacy Study Group have completed. These studies include an exhaustive review of labeling claims and are made for drugs marketed under new drug and antibiotic drug procedures between 1938 and 1962 (Just make sure you want 1938 to 1962 to refer to the drugs that were marketed.

Good Automated Manufacturing Practice (GAMP) [89]

ISPE Gamp

On Tuesday, February 25, 2003, the FDA cited (Guide for Validation of Automated Systems, GAMP) as an "Industry Reference" GAMP specializes in

1. Basic Principles of Computerized Systems Compliance
2. A Risk-based Approach to Compliant GxP Computerized Systems

---

[89] (Krause et al., 2004)

3. Part 11 - Risk Management
4. Good Practice Guide Electronic Records and Signatures Principles
5. Practical Application of Computerized Systems Compliance
6. A Risk-Based Approach to GxP Process Control Systems

International Organization for Standardization Section 14971 (ISO 14971) [90]

ISO 14971 refers to a set of international standards guiding guides manufacturers on how to identify the amount of contamination that has accrued and how to contain the hazards associated with medical devices. The FDA endorses ISO 14971 as an acceptable risk management model for the United States. FDA believes that sufficient domestic and international guidelines are available to provide assistance to manufacturers for the validation of software and risk analysis.

International Society for Pharmaceutical Engineering (ISPE) [91]

ISPE is a global, not-for-profit volunteer society of technical professionals who apply their expertise in the regulated healthcare manufacturing industries. Companies and organizations involved in ISP activities include pharmaceuticals, biotechnologies, medical devices, bulk/intermediates, diagnostic manufacturers, architect/engineer/construction firms, government agencies, universities, equipment manufacturers, and suppliers.

---

[90] (ANSI,2007)
[91] (ISPE , 2017)

Created in partnership with the FDA, ISPE's Baseline Guides offer practical answers to the complex, dynamic challenges facing facility designers today. In addition to providing an understanding of products and processes, they also offer an outline of architectural and utility systems needed to meet government requirements. Additionally, they address GMP and non-GMP regulations and detail facility commissioning and qualification.

Chapter 6

Data Environments

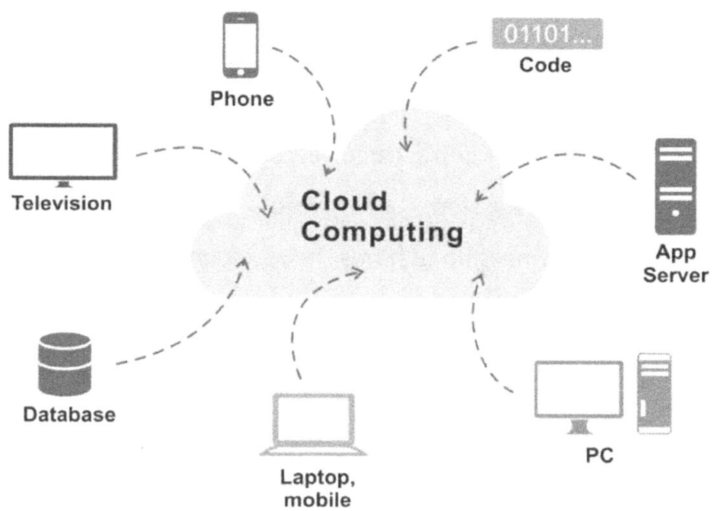

Regulatory agencies are concerned about how data under their jurisdiction is being processed. We may see ourselves as technical computer geeks, provisioners of Infrastructure, software, and applications services but, regulatory authorities see controlled and uncontrolled data. They take a look at your controls and determine if you have the ability to manage a regulated environment. If the data that's being hosted is subject to regulations then, it needs to be handled accordingly.

Cloud computing gives users the ability to buy IT from a new consumption model. The model is not a traditional storefront in which the buyer meets the seller face to face. The model is one in which there may be thousands of middlemen who handle the information before you access it.

Managing a cloud facility is not easy. Operational issues can vary from the allocation of resources, customer complaints, technical problems, and infrastructure changes. Managers of cloud services are challenged with ensuring that the facilities design yields optimal network performance, infrastructure cost is kept under control, and future strategy, mission, and vision meet system scalability requirements. Ownership defines how much stake you have in a process.

The question we need to ask is, who has ownership and control over the original data, copies of the data and modifications made to the data. If the owner of the data would like to have it deleted, does he have to notify everyone upstream or downstream? If you have a clear picture of the type of information generated by your business, the region you plan to do business in, and the regulations that govern your activities then we can shift our focus and take a look at the environment that houses your data.

Ownership includes not just providing access to data but creating new forms of information, altering, packaging, storing, deleting and even selling data. In most cases, the owner has the authority to apply restrictions and specific controls over certain data types. The owner can assign these controls to additional parties.

Who has custody of the data and where did they get this jurisdiction. The question that we need to ask is who owns, controls or administers the environment which the data flows from and through, and what point does custody over the data ends, and another network administrator assumes control. I have listed four data environments. Each environment has specific controls that must be put in place to satisfy specific business objectives.

1. Non-Regulated Data Environment
2. User-Managed Regulated-Environment
3. User/SP-Managed Regulated-Environment
4. SP-Managed Regulated-Environment

Non-Regulated Data Environment

The Non-Regulated Data environment does not contain regulated data. In this environment, you are not facilitating or creating information that requires regulating. This environment receives the standard servicing activities from the service provider. A standard service agreement that meets your required level of service is sufficient..

User-Managed Regulated-Environment

The User-Managed Regulated-Environment contains Regulated data that is being managed by the user. In this environment, the service provider provides a workspace for the client to play in. The service provider or client may or may not provide an image or specifications for the hardware and software and qualify the environment. The Service Provider qualifies the connection. The user is responsible for ensuring that the proper procedures, governance, and resources are in place.

User/SP-Managed Regulated-Environment

The User/SP-Managed Regulated-Environment contains Regulated Data that is being managed by the User/SP. This a hybrid environment in which the Service Provider (SP) and the User share the responsibility of ensuring that the proper procedures, governance, resources, and quality oversight are in place. The responsibilities need to be clearly defined.

SP-Managed Regulated-Environment

The SP-Managed Regulated-Environment contains regulated data that's being managed by the service provider. The service provider will manage the environment and ensure that the proper procedures, governance, resources, and quality oversight are in place.

Detailed look into the environments

From a regulatory perspective, there are only two main types of data environments (regulated and non-regulated) being hosted by service providers. Either you have controlled data, which require regulatory oversight or you do not. Nonregulated information typically defaults to statistical controls for improving the Quality of Service(QOS). However for the sake of gaining a better understanding of the of individual responsibilities we have listed four environments. Except for the non-regulated environment, every environment contains additional activities that help maintain control. At the end of the day, it does not matter who manages the instance but how the instance is being managed. If the proper resources procedural, technical, and administrative controls with Quality oversight are not in place to ensure security, privacy and integrity then all of our work is in vain. All of the environments have measurable controls in place to prevent illegal access for misuse but, the regulated environments require additional activities as defined by regulatory agencies.

Regardless of the environment, at a minimum, every service level agreement should contain verbiage about the terms of service and the nondisclosure of information. Before an SLA is developed an assessment should be completed to uncover what types of data being managed and how data flows through your environment. A detailed data map the shows all of the interfaces, conversions, translations, and, reports must be developed. This assessment should be conducted in the light of the guidance, policies, and laws where the information is being pushed and pulled from. A risk profile and data flow strategies should be developed that is reflective of known or potential incidents and threats.

A set of policies and procedures that establishes the rules of engagement for data and information must be developed. The approach should include information on how to manage data ownership throughout the lifecycle, with strong consideration for the design, operation, maintenance, defects, events, and corrective actions.

An audit should be initiated on a periodic basis. Develop an SLA with your needs in mind, and that is not driven by an industry standard. Depending upon your needs the content of a service level agreement can vary. Your service-level agreement should be measurable. There should be mechanisms built into the agreement that protects the user and the contact service provider if the terms of the agreement cannot be met. Rules or responsibilities of the contract service provider, client, and any third-party integrator must be clearly defined. Any procurement, security or maintenance standards that will affect the performance of your cloud computing experience must be agreed upon. How the contract service provider processes, preserves and retains your data must be defined. Ensure that your contract service provider has the right storage, search, collection, and handling and preservation procedures in place for locating valuable information.

Non-Regulated Data Environment

The Non-Regulated Data Environment does not contain information that must adhere to specific regulatory controls. In this environment, you are not working with products or services that require adherence to specific regulations. The information in this environment receives the standard servicing activities as defined in the Service Level Agreement (SLA). The expectations for this environment is being managed by the Quality of Service (QOS) offerings of your compliance department.

For the most part, the goals in this environment are to achieve maximum bandwidth capacity while at the same time managining network performance elements like latency, error rate, and uptime. This environment receives the standard servicing activities from the service provider contained in any Service level agreement. The maintenance activities include things like an event, incident and problem management and detection, backup and restores, login issues, bugs and hotfixes, IP allocation, operating system tuning, availability CPU, memory and storage resources, and more. Unless specifically requested there is no need to apply additional controls if there are not any regulated records in this environment. If we are not creating, modifying, maintaining, archiving, retrieving, or transmitting any regulated records(s), then we are not required to demonstrate compliance with regulatory agencies.

The Non-Regulated Data Environment is most likely to be a Public Cloud infrastructure where infrastructure resources (hardware, software, compute power) are accessible to the public or a large industry group. This is a shared multi-customer infrastructure with secure isolation. An environment where all resources are shared within a single network context and services are First to come first served. The Service Level Agreement ("SLA") is the governing agreement between the service provider and the user. This arrangement is purely device-based. The agreement is all about the use of the facility and the bandwidth. The cloud provider may have extensive experience supporting clients but will not be responsible for supporting regulated activities outside of standard service offerings. The cloud provider is not responsible for providing any regulatory controls beyond commitments expressed in the standard service agreement (SLA). This may include 24x7 management of servers, operating systems, storage, web, application and or database software, networking and other required infrastructure found in a service provider datacenter. The SLA may go further and provide:

1. VMware for web-based management: for monitoring compute, network and storage capacity
2. Multi-layered security: allows the combination of multiple mitigating security controls to protect resources and data
3. Management of virtual servers: Whereas server (computer and various server programs) at someone else's location that is shared by multiple Web site owners so that each owner can

use and administer it as though they had complete control of the server.

4. Ability to Manage CPU, memory, storage capacity, IP addresses
5. Load balancing for virtual hardware to distribute network and application traffic across different servers to improve the concurrent user capacity and overall reliability
6. The firewall in the form of the computer system or network for blocking unauthorized access while permitting outward communication
7. Backup and monitoring, patching systems
8. Operating system Unix, UnixWare, VectorLinux, and Windows.
9. Incident Management: monitoring and detection of security events

In this scenario system access may be controlled by the user, but the SP is responsible for the facilitation of electronic records that are being managed by the system.

User-Managed Regulated-Environment

This environment contains regulated data that is being managed by the user. In this environment, users can colocate or rent server space and other computing hardware form the service provider. The service provider provides a workplace for the user to play in and the necessary utilities for creating a virtual environment. The user places their hardware and software into the virtual environment. In this scenario, the cloud provider qualifies the connection to the user's equipment. This environment contains the same bells and whistle as defined by the standard SLA in Non-Regulated Data Environment. In this environment, the service provider may or may not qualify the user's components. It is the responsibility of the user to purchase equipment that meets the service providers specifications and applicable regulatory requirements. Sometimes the service provider will lease equipment and system images to the user because the components must conform to specific throughput, elasticity and scalability requirements of the SP. The User is responsible for ensuring that the proper procedures, governance, resources, and quality oversight are in place to protect the accuracy, reliability, integrity, availability, authenticity, confidentiality, of the regulated records.

The user is in no way an expert at how the service provider creates policies and procedures for managing and provisioning services. Typically the service providers processes are loosely implemented to accommodate many different types of environments. If the user requires a regulated environment and the service provider can not meet the requirements, the user should not force the service provider to provision service that's not in their paradigm. Nor should they try to entice the Service provider to package services that are out of their paradigm. If the service provider does not have a methodology in place for compliant practices its more than likely, they will need some time to assess their infrastructure and leverage outside expertise to help them understand the requirements put on them by regulatory agencies and auditing organizations.

In the case of service providers who understand regulatory compliance, the user should rely on their expertise and as tempting as it may be, try not to control their activities. It would be advantageous to the user if they could leverage the service provider's procedures as long as the procedures are aligned with their processes. The user needs to audit the service provider's environment to make sure their practices are brought into line with regulatory and industry expectations. If the assessment or audit is favorable, then the user can leverage their expertise to achieve a compliant solution.

Always remember that whoever manages the data must comply with the regulations governing the data. Beware of service providers who desire to sell you services that claim to make you compliant. Most of them are selling out of the box-automated or semi-configured solutions. Some of the solutions are secure and technologically sound, however; security requirements are only a part of what is needed for a company to be officially compliant. Purchasing is the easy part. Once a solution is purchased, it must be integrated into your environment.

At best, the service provider can offer an application containing compliance elements that are built into the functionality of the system. They are selling a compliant system with all of the bells and whistles already integrated into the software package thats on the shelf. Technical controls such as limited access, audit trail, operational system checks, authority checks, device checks, and network monitoring, can be easily purchased off the shelf. However, can a computer evaluate policy changes that are governed by regulations? Can you take years of quality experience and put them in a computer to replace you Quality Department. Can a computer act as a change control board. No! The computer has no common sense. This is one of the reasons why the system must be thoroughly integrated into the business groups that interact with it.

It is not possible for any vendor to offer a turnkey compliant system for a regulated environment unless the vendor assumes the responsibilities of managing your company. The vendor must clearly understand the regulations that govern your business activities. For companies to be compliant with regulatory agencies, they must know the laws that affect your operations. You cannot implement appropriate security controls if you are not aware of the type of information generated by your business, the region you plan to do business in, and the regulations that govern your activities. Without this information, how could any company know what type of system to build.

Most managers do a great job purchasing state of the art computer monitoring packages that get the job done but fail miserably on getting consensus from the entire stakeholder community on how the job should get done. The solution must be thoroughly integrated it into the organization framework so they can verify its effectiveness.

The User-Managed Regulated-Environment contains all of the servicing elements contained in the non-regulated environment and additional controls to ensure that regulated data is protected. These controls must not be blindly implemented but based on a risk-based approach and a documented design, whose software has been thoroughly tested and accompanied by procedures. Verification must exist proving that the environment conforms to technical requirements and that it works as intended. In this environment, the cloud provider will provide a limited guarantee that the infrastructure will perform as intended. However, it is up to the users to provide additional controls for creating, modifying, maintaining, archiving, retrieving, or transmitting any electronic records(s). The User is responsible for providing security for information that resides on the system. Each contract is different. In this environment The service provider may be responsible for ensuring that the environment has been qualified as a standard service. The User-Managed Regulated-Environment is an ideal solution for most Quality and Compliance departments. Even though the electronic records are being housed offsite, it is still being managed by onsite personnel. The operation and maintenance of the system are still subject to the user's Quality oversight. The records would receive no less maintenance as if it were onsite. The User-Managed Regulated-Environment may look like:

SLA

- ✓ VMware for web based management: for monitoring compute, network and storage capacity
- ✓ Multi layered security: allows the combination of multiple mitigating security controls to protect resources and data.
- ✓ Manage virtual servers: Whereas server (computer and various server programs) at someone else's location that is shared by multiple Web site owners so that each owner can use and administer it as though they had complete control of the server.
- ✓ Manage CPU, memory, storage capacity, IP addresses
- ✓ Load balancing for virtual hardware to distribute network and/or application traffic across different servers to improve the concurrent user capacity and overall reliability
- ✓ Firewall in the form of computer system or network for blocking unauthorized access while permitting outward communication.
- ✓ Procedures for archive, Backup & restore, disaster and recovery, and monitoring, patching systems, etc.
- ✓ Operating system Unix, UnixWare, VectorLinux, Windows.
- ✓ Address: events incident, problems

Additional Controls

System and process procedures, document management for system documentation, audits, change control, corrective action preventive action, inspections, metrics and management reviews, deviation, documented investigation of (events incident, problems), risk management, training, validation, SDLC process, investigations, regulatory compliance, complaints, QA, vender management are managed by the user.

These are the minimum requirements that must be put in place to ensure compliance with regulations and to ensure control over processes used for hosting regulated information. The implementation should take into account the impact the system will have on your ability to access and retain your information.

User/Service Provider-Managed Regulated-Environment

User/SP-Managed Regulated-Environment is a hybrid environment in which the SP and the client shares the responsibility of managing the space. Both groups are responsible for ensuring that the proper controls are in place. In this hybrid-hosting environment, the user may want the cloud provider to manage the activities for maintaining the performance of the system.

The user wants a compliant environment to conduct business but may not have the resources for fully managing the new environment. Traditionally, for most externally managed services, after an audit of the vender has been approved, the users are willing to let the vender manage certain aspects of the system. The user is willing to have the SP manage critical data management activities but reserves the right to reject or apply final approval on all critical decisions. From our earlier discussion, regulatory agencies agree that the most important factor in classifying who has control over a system is whether the persons responsible for the content of the information on the system control access to the system. Well, in this scenario, the cloud provider may be legally responsible for the accuracy of electronic records that are on the system as well as access to the system.

Cloud computing technology can conform too many different service models that can be used to deliver a plethora of services. The SLA describes the responsibilities of all parties and the level of Quality of service expected as well as the ranges of services provided. In this complex environment, services must be provisioned based upon the service level agreement. The SLA defines the way that services are being rendered and the way theses service are prioritized. It sets the expectations in the service provider/user relationship by describing what services are being provided and who is responsible for delivering those services. It also defines what repercussions are if the level of services is compromised.

The SLA is not static but changes with the types of service and products acquired over time. The SLA may be dependent upon a multi-layer agreement where the service provider has an agreement with the platform provider who has an agreement with the infrastructure provider who has an agreement with the application provider who has an agreement with the software development company. Disclosure is key to developing an SLA. Define the level of service you want from your provider and your vendor, especially if the vendor is responsible for maintaining the performance of the system.

Most service plans of this complexity give the service provider management authority over the infrastructure while the user handles the rest.

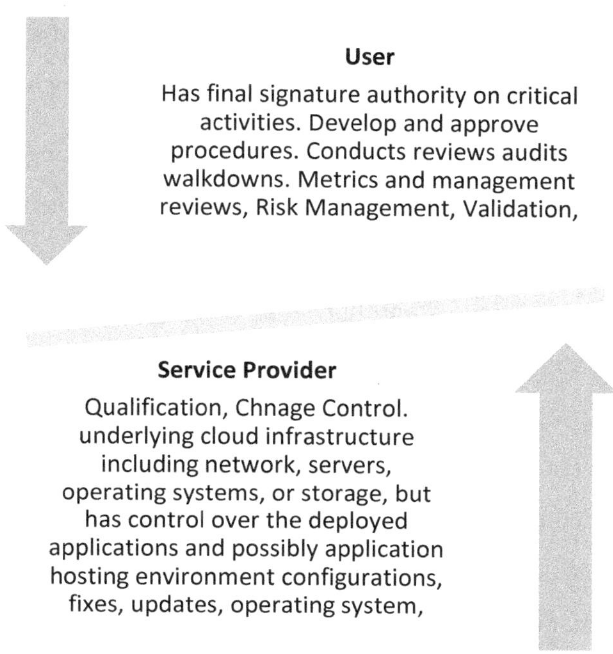

In this environment, the service provider may add value to the services being provided by the system by assessing its quality or the quality of the environment where the information resides. For example; the client may want The cloud provider to collect data for system access. Information such as who, when, and what the user's employees are accessing is compiled by the cloud provider and made visible to the client. Most regulations require that the administrator of the system maintain an access history for all controlled information. Because the CSP is monitoring access for the user, are they held responsible for developing the procedures and defining organizational activities supporting those records? Monitoring security may require service providers to field audits and inspections from regulatory agencies because they have become an extension of the user and are storing security documents that are controlled by regulatory agencies.

If there is any incriminating evidence of wrongdoing that can be traced back to the lack of scrutiny for system access, then the SP can be held liable for criminal activity or financial restitution. The additional controls offer us another layer of protection. The service provider must show evidence of how are restrictions implemented to guarantee how data is processed. That is why it is so important to have the proper controls. Procedural controls, technical controls, administrative controls, and organizational structure all play a role in ensuring the transparency, confidentiality integrity, and availability of personal information.

The SP and the user share in the services offered but have unique responsibilities in determining the quality of the service. Both parties are responsible for providing leadership for the following activities. Your SLA might include verbiage surrounding:

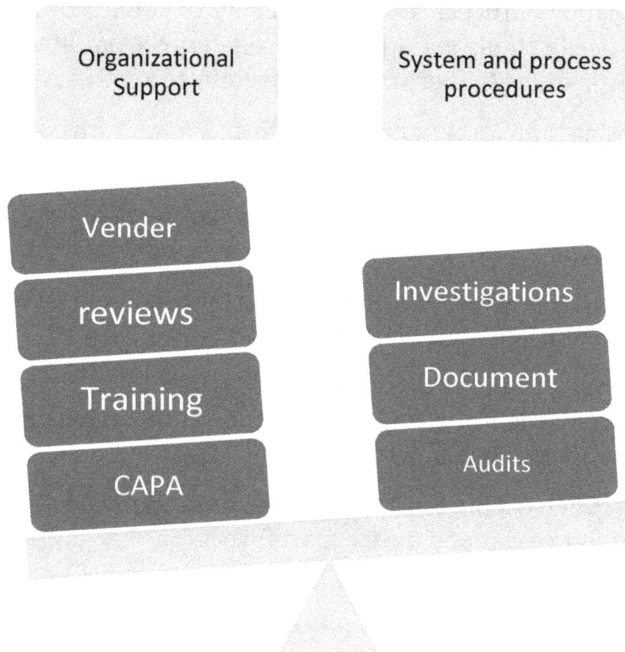

1. Qualification/Validation: Who's responsible for proving by the regulations develop the procedure, process, equipment, fixes, and bugs or verifying the system works correctly as designed.
2. Organizational Support: Who will pay for the human resources needed to complete the below Quality System task such as deviations, CAPA, change Controls, audits, investigations, and document storage.
3. System and process procedures: Who's responsible for developing and communicating changes in procedures and processes
4. Metrics and Management Reviews: What metrics needs to be put in place to determine the effectiveness of the relationship?
5. Risk Management Are the differences in how each party views risk. Is risk regulatory, security, or business driven?
6. Training Management: Who manages the training for the relationship? Which curriculum is being used to define the amount of training necessary?

7. Investigations process: Does the Quality of service or inability to meet specifications initiate an investigation? What are the levels of investigations that drive commensurate corrective actions?
8. Purchasing and Acceptance Activities: What is the system for managing ASP activities, hardware, and software?
9. Equipment and Calibration: What is the System for qualifying equipment and software, devices, and instruments in the cloud?
10. Document Control/ Document Management: Is the Document Management process documented?
11. Corrective Action, Preventive Action (CAPA): Do you have Corrective Action and Preventive Action (CAPA), root cause, risk assesments to mitigate incidents.
12. Change Control: Do you have a system for managing changes to devices, processes and device master records
13. Training Management: Do you have a system for ensuring that users, vendors, DBAs, and clients are trained
14. Design Controls: Do you have a system for system for implementing processes and changes to existing designs
15. Audit Management According to GLP GCP GMP Regulations: Do you have a system for documented independent inspection and review
16. Customer Complaints: Do you have a system for system in place for managing customer, client feedback
17. Supplier Management:

Service Provider-Managed Regulated-Environment

Service provider-Managed Regulated-Environment is popular where infrastructure costs make new initiatives cost prohibitive. In this environment, the user is responsible for auditing the service provider. The user must ensure that the proper controls are in place and the environment is being managed in accordance with regulatory expectations. The service provider must show capabilities that include but are not limited:

1. To establish, implement and maintain a set of processes that provides a product and/or service with the system attributes appropriate to meet the needs of the user, regulatory authorities and internal customers.
2. To develop and use effective monitoring and control systems for process performance and product quality, thereby providing assurance of continued suitability and capability of processes. Quality risk management can be useful in establishing the monitoring and control system.
3. To identify and implement appropriate product quality improvements, process improvements, variability reduction, innovations, and pharmaceutical quality system enhancements, thereby increasing the ability to consistently

The service provider is responsible for ensuring that the proper procedures, governance, resources, and quality system are in place to protect the accuracy, integrity, and transparency, of the process. The user must have final approval for all critical decisions.

There should be documentation specifying their quality management system and a clear set of objectives to translate the quality policy and strategies into measurable activities. Service provider's Quality Management should be focused on setting quality objectives, operational processes and related resources to fulfill the quality objectives. These responsibilities should be assigned to those who are in direct control of the company and reside at the highest levels of authority and accountability. These individuals should have the authority to mobilize resources within the company or site. Senior management must ensure a state of control which provides assurance of continued process performance and product quality.

Senior management has the ultimate responsibility to ensure an effective quality system is in place, and that responsibilities and authorities are defined, communicated and implemented throughout the company. A Quality Manual or equivalent documentation approach should be established and should contain the description of the service provider's quality system. The description should include:

1. Management Review: Senior management should be responsible for quality system governance through management review to ensure its continuing suitability and effectiveness. Management should assess the conclusions of periodic reviews of process performance and product quality.
2. Resource Management: Management should determine and provide adequate and appropriate resources (human, financial, materials, facilities and equipment) to implement and maintain the quality system and continually improve its effectiveness.
3. Internal Communication: Management should ensure appropriate communication processes are established and implemented within the organization.

A company can outsource activities at all stages of the product lifecycle. The pharmaceutical quality system, including the management responsibilities described in this section, extends to the oversight and review of outsourced activities. Normally under a contract, the contract giver should be responsible for assessing the suitability and competence of the contract acceptor to Pharmaceutical Quality System carry out the work required.

1. Quality Planning: As part of quality planning, senior management should ensure the quality objectives needed to implement the quality policy are defined and communicated.

2. Quality Policy: Senior management should establish a quality policy that describes the overall intentions and direction of the company related to quality.
3. Management Commitment: Senior management has the ultimate responsibility to ensure an effective pharmaceutical quality system is in place, and that responsibilities and authorities are

It is SPs management's responsibility to establish an organization whose goal is to implement and maintain a set of processes that provide a product with the quality attributes appropriate to meet the needs of external customers, regulatory authorities, and internal customers. This organization will develop and use effective monitoring and control various quality management systems for process performance and product quality. Management with executive responsibility is responsible for developing and fostering an organizational structure that is committed to quality. The structure of the organization must be clearly defined.

An organizational chart that explains the interrelationships and responsibilities of each department and how it is expected to function must be developed. Leadership must be established within the organization that empowers its members to assess the human and financial resources, workflow activities to complete the task at hand. The companies Vision, goals, mission and organizational expectations must be communicated to everyone. The organization must be appropriately resourced for the task at hand. Employees must be trained and properly managed to perform their responsibilities. Resources must be in place for performing required activities. Communication tools and training must be in place for employees to achieve the organizational structure's commitment to its objectives and quality goals.

A plan that includes a high-level strategy of how management is going to achieve its goals must be put in place. The plan must be inclusive of policies, standards, procedures, and quality practices. The plan should also explain how the interrelationships and responsibilities of each department is expected to its goals

Chapter 7

System Access

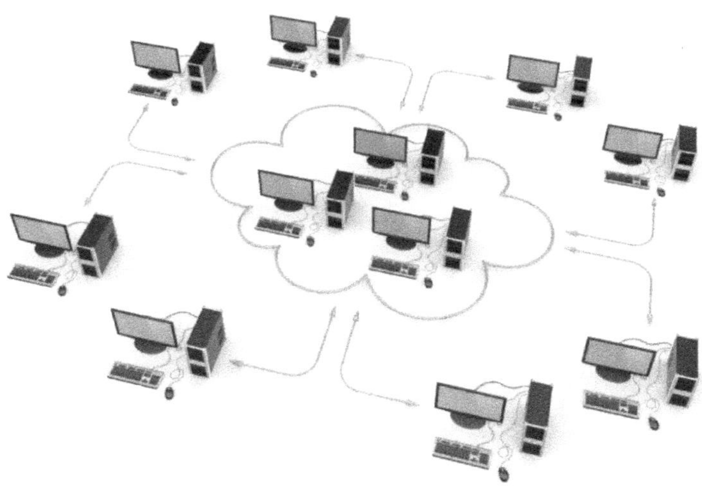

Hosting Environments

Most business applications run in a myriad of physical and virtual environments. Thus, cloud environments are very dynamic in nature. Cloud platforms can be easily configured to dynamically allocate IT resources to applications, perform load balancing based on resource consumption levels as well as perform dynamic power management to cut down power costs.

Within the Shared Hosting Environment, you share server infrastructure resources with others. However, Each client has complete access to their account within the environment. The host's responsibility stops at the creation of an isolated environment, fast connection and operating platform. In this environment, the user manages everything from their end. The user becomes the virtual system administrator with the power to create, customize, clone and provision virtual machines (VMs), and quickly increase or decrease capacity to match changing demands.

In the Managed Hosting Environment, the hosting company actively manages various elements of your space. Some hosting companies are contracted to maintenance the environment. Within a datacenter, the hosting company can update software content and design elements, manage servers, operating systems, storage, web, application and database software, networking and other required infrastructure changes. You will not have to share dedicated server with anyone else. Each virtual machine will have an isolated virtual storage location and will be fully isolated from other virtual machines on the server. The Managed Hosting environment is very flexible. It can satisfy the customer's requirement and comfortably accommodate complex customized solutions, beyond the capabilities of what traditional Cloud infrastructures can support.

Software security flaws can be introduced at any stage of the software development lifecycle. Security flaws can occur as a result as failing to identify security requirements up front, creating conceptual designs that have logic errors, using poor coding practices that introduce technical vulnerabilities, deploying the software improperly, and improper maintenance or updating can lead to serious breaches. Setting aside software and hardware issues, we must ask ourselves how can we minimize leaks and stop criminals from stealing information.

When we talk about privacy, it is nice to understand that many countries have their unique definition of privacy. For the sake of this book, we will define privacy an aspect of information technology (IT) that focuses on an organization or individual ability to determine what data in a computer system can be shared with third parties. Just because your system is secure and isolated does not mean you achieved privacy. Privacy does not necessarily mean isolation. You can have a deployment of security applications such as anti-virus, logging, authentication, single sign-on, authorization, device profiling, encryption, alerting, and malware detection and not met privacy requirements. Security without privacy is a design flaw.

Your concept of privacy may not meet privacy policy standards to someone else. Most countries have unwritten norms that govern the handling of personal Data. Most of these standards also have some form of breach notification statutes in place to protect against breaches of sensitive information.

When your data flows outside of the countries boundaries where you conduct your business, you have to ask yourself, what compliance requirements govern the handling of data for that region, what laws do you have to conform to that would guarantee data privacy. For starters, your privacy level agreement should define what forms of data is expected to be under the protection and how it should be handled. What level of service or guarantees should you expect from your service provider or what governance is in place to ensure that data privacy and leaking of information does not take place? In the absence of laws, your critical, confidential and private information could be shared, sold and in some cases stolen without your knowledge. There are laws and general expectations in place that govern the usage of information in most regions but once you step outside of the legal coverage, your information enters into the wild west.

It is not wise to trust just any service provide with your critical information. Some pirate will move your information to a region will the laws are lax and enforcement is weak. Most users expect their data to be kept within the domain of the laws governing it. However, with the need to centralize global IT systems, many service providers are consolidating flow into less condense traffic areas where optimization is maximized, and laws and regulation are less restrictive. Strong security guarantees that data's integrity is maintained. It ensures data is not corrupted or accessed by unauthorized individuals or parties. Data security gives you the confidence that the information is accurate and reliable and is available for agencies and users.

Data privacy, on the other hand, is all about the measurements of trust. For data, privacy information must be suitably defined and used by agreed purposes. Entities like the Federal Trade Commission enforces penalties against companies that have negated to ensure the privacy of a customer's data. Companies are not expected to disclosed, rent or sell information that was entrusted to them to third parties without getting prior approval. The service provider should provide some written commitment to adhere to privacy restrictions. With a degree of assurance, They must give some type of guarantee that data is being kept out of the hands of un-trusted sources.

This is why it is so important to have the proper controls in place to guarantee a well-controlled environment. Government regulations, administrative, policies, guidelines, work instructions, manuals, protocols, templates and various safeguards, technical controls, and a well defined Quality System all play a role in ensuring the transparency, confidentiality integrity, privacy, security, and availability of private, confidential, and critical information.

Cloud Management

The most important factor in determining the level of security required for your system starts by classifying it as open or closed. Is the system accessible for public use or closed for your teams use? According to 21 CFR Part 11, the definition of a closed system is an environment in which system access is controlled by persons who are responsible for the content of electronic records that are on the system. In other words, your system administrators should consist of the same staff who provide maintenance for your systems records. It dosent matter if your IT staff is located onsite, somewhere in Africa or online, as long as they are under your governance, the location where they reside is inconsequential. If system access is controlled by individuals who are responsible for the content of the records on the system, then theoretically you will have a governance theme that's weaved into the fabric of your policies, guidelines, work instructions, manuals, protocols, templates, safeguards, and technical controls. Administrators and users will view your processes using the same methodology and approach. Your IT procedures for change control, deviations, backup and restore disaster and recovery, and archiving process is sanctioned by the same senior management and enforced by the Quality team.

If you are outsourcing your network to an external organization who is not part of your organization nor an extension of your management team then your system is considered open. Your system is seen as extremely vulnerable because your network is not under your managements umbrella of controls.

NIST provides general characteristics expected from four types of deployment models. These models are not all conclusive, but they give us a basic Cloud framework to build upon. Take the time to ask, what Cloud model have you experienced and who manages the content and access of records on your system.

1. Public Cloud. The cloud infrastructure is made available to the general public or a large industry group and is owned by an organization selling cloud services.
2. Private Cloud: The cloud infrastructure is operated solely for an organization. It may be managed by the organization or a third party and may exist on premise or off premise.
3. Community Cloud: The cloud infrastructure is shared by several organizations and supports a specific community that has shared concerns It may be managed by the organizations or a third party and may exist on premise or off premise.
4. Hybrid Cloud. The cloud infrastructure is a composition of two or more clouds (private, community, or public) that remain unique entities but are bound together by standardized or proprietary technology that enables data and application portability (e.g., cloud bursting for load-balancing between clouds).

If If the vendor is an extended part of your team and is following your access procedures or is under your governance, then your system is considered closed. Records on the system are supposedly considered less vulnerable to theft or tampering and only need minimal security controls. The is true because, IT governance is being promulgated from a central source. In theory, records in a closed system are centrally managed and supposedly receive a single set of directives from senior management. If the Vender has good practices in place for managing the content and access of records on the system, then the parent company can rely on the vender's policies and procedures to ensure security and privacy.

However, if a vendor's system administrator provides access to the system but is not tied to the same organizational relationship with those who manage the content of the records on the system, then the system is considered an Open System. This is true because, the client's polices and approcahes to security, privacy, policies and commitment to quality may not necessarily align. The vendor may have the philosophy that Quality of service be statistically driven. So, their approach to solving problems is through assessing and implementing process improvements and risk analysis. Such things like change control can be automated and carried out with little to none administrative oversight. The less the risk, the fewer security that's needed.

The client, on the other hand, believes that quality is driven by following regulatory requirements. So when regulatory agencies demand that a change control board be put in place to evaluate changes and their impact, then it must be done. If the system intends to handle regulated information, then it must conform to regulatory requirements. Those responsible for the content of the records and access management would need to take additional measures to protect information from being tampered with, stolen, or deleted.

In the Public Cloud, cloud infrastructure is made available to the general public or a large industry group and is owned by an organization selling cloud services. Public Clouds have a multi-customer infrastructure

a) Shared multi-customer infrastructure
b) Secure isolation between customers
c) Less administrative burden
d) All resources are shared
e) Single network context
f) Public transport only
g) First come first served
h) One–size-fits-all, No customization

In the Private Cloud, infrastructure is operated solely for an organization. It may be managed by the organization or a third party and may exist on premise or off premise.

a) Private secure network.
b) Dedicated to a single tenant (user environment)
c) Greater control (Security, Compliance, QoS)
d) More expensive to deploy, manage and maintain

Virtual Private Cloud: The cloud infrastructure is operated solely for an organization. It may be managed by the organization or a third party and may exist on premise or off premise. It is allocated within a public cloud environment, but provides a certain level of isolation

a) Shared, multi-tenant environment
b) Provides infrastructure computing resources (CPU, memory, disk) on demand.
c) Logical segmentation of resources
d) Private Compute pools
e) Private network integration
f) Dedicated address space
g) Dedicated firewall context

h) Addresses more complex needs of enterprise customers (e.g. security, networking, service desk support, etc).
i) Guaranteed availability
j) Fully auditable

Hybrid Cloud: Hybrid Cloud is a private cloud that is interoperable with other public or private clouds. The cloud infrastructure is a composition of two or more clouds (private, community, or public) that remain unique entities but are bound together by standardized or proprietary technology that enables data and application portability (e.g., cloud bursting for load-balancing between clouds).

a) Customer leverages 'what they have' in conjunction with the cloud
b) Leveraging existing assets and applications
c) Secure linkage to outside cloud services

Community Cloud: In a Community Cloud the cloud infrastructure is shared by several organizations and supports a specific community that has shared concerns It may be managed by the organizations or a third party and may exist on premise or off premise.

Regional Considerations

Do you plan on doing business in North America, South America, Europe, or Asia-Pacific. If you do then you might want to take the time to find out which regions have cloud enabled repositories and which regions are planning to have third party vendors manage their data. Find out which service providers and data centers are located in the area you plan to conduct business. The location which you plan to do business must take into consideration the current regulations. The regulatory requirements will help you develop an appropriate design.

Complete an assessment of your products and services and ask yourself, what services are you providing or what are you selling? The region in which you do business will determine which laws you should follow. Each country, economic power, and the political entity have their brand of regulations. If you plan to do business in multiple countries, it would be a good idea to find out if there any harmonized practices there. In the midst of an ever expanding industry where guidance, standards, policies, and practices are ever evolving, we can be assured that regulatory governance isn't going anywhere. With the shortage of government funding, some agencies rely on levies and fines as a source of funding. This may serve as an extra incentive for executing the law. Enforcing regulations is one of the regulatory agency's highest priorities.

Without effective regulatory oversight and enforcement, some businesses will disregard even the clearest regulations or will not be adequately vigilant to ensure compliance with the law, potentially disclosing confidential information thus, harming the publics trust. Effective enforcement also ensures that businesses remain vigilant about their corporate responsibility to comply with the laws being enforced. Firms must invest in proper procedures, governance, resources, and quality system to ensure the transparency, confidentiality integrity, and availability of confidential information and trust isn't broken. Most localities have laws governing the collection, protection, maintenance and notification when personal data is breached. These regulations are in place to prevent harm to the public. Regulatory agencies are quickly becoming an integral part of a complex and globalized Information System. Their expectations are being ingrained into the fabric of business ethics. It is imperative that you develop strong relationships with your regulatory partners. This relationship helps to build strong infrastructure, that is sustainable.

Regulatory Applicability

Make sure your business partners and vendors have a complete understanding of the technical and legal framework that govern the processing of your electronic information. What activities surrounding your product or service are regulatory applicable. There is no question that the primary attribute that companies are looking for in cloud computation is security. However, from a regulatory standpoint, the number one concern from regulators is the protection and integrity of regulated information. If I were to list of cloud concerns in the order of importance from a business perspective, it would be system security, personal protection, and national security. If I listed it from a consumer driven regulatory framework the order of it would be rearranged to personal protection, security, and national security. Likewise in some circles, national security is considered a primary directive. In certain situations, National security directives trumps over, personal protection and security. Take the time to detarmine the types of information that is being housed in your domain. Undestand how it flows through your netwrok. Set up gates to direct critical, sensitive, private, confidential into their appropriate space.

HIPPA[92]

Information your doctors, nurses, and other health care providers put in medical record including conversations your doctor has about care or treatment with nurses and others and stored information in the health insurer's computer system and billing systems at the clinic is protected under U.S laws. All entities must put in place safeguards to protect your health information and ensure they

---

[92] (HHS, 2013)

do not use or disclose your health information improperly. Covered entities must reasonably limit uses and disclosures to the minimum necessary to accomplish their intended purpose. Entities must have procedures in place to limit who can view and access your health information as well as implement training programs for employees about how to protect your health information. This law is includes all venders and business associates. Business associates must put in place safeguards to protect your health information and ensure they do not use or disclose your health information improperly.

HHS' Office for Civil Rights (OCR) is responsible for enforcing the Privacy and Security Rules. OCR works in conjunction with the Department of Justice (DOJ) to refer possible criminal violations of HIPAA. The Rule strikes a balance that permits important uses of information, while protecting the privacy of people who seek care and healing. The HIPAA Privacy regulations require health care providers and organizations, as well as their business associates, develop and follow procedures that ensure the confidentiality and security of protected health information (PHI) when it is transferred, received, handled, or shared. This applies to all forms of PHI, including paper, oral, and electronic.

European Union's (EU's) Directive on Data Protection[93]

Under EU law, persons or organizations that collect and manage your personal information must protect it from misuse. Personal data can only be gathered legally under strict conditions, for a

---

[93] (EUR-Lex, 1995)

legitimate purpose. The directive outlaws disclosure of any personal details held by a European company to any foreign entities that do not meet the EU's data safeguard guidelines (the basis of various efforts to meet EU standards, such as the United States' Safe Harbor program)

Canada's Personal Information Protection and Electronic Documents Act (PIPEDA)[94]

PIPEDA define how private sector organizations may collect, use or disclose personal information in the course of commercial activities. PIPEDA gives individuals the right to access and request correction of the personal information these organizations may have collected about them.

Stored Communications Act[95]

Stored Communication Act (SCA) provides adequate privacy safeguards for individuals' electronic communications. SCA creates a broad bar against service providers voluntarily disclosing a customer's communications to the government or other entities and second, it establishes procedures under which the government can require a provider to disclose customers' communications or records. It governs, for instance, when the government can demand that Google turn over e-mail s; when social media sites like Facebook must provide private posts; when video-sharing sites like YouTube must provide stored videos; and when cell phone companies must turn over cell location

---

[94] (PIPEDA, 2016)
[95] (US Government Printing Office, 2010)

information. There are two conditions in which the communication is protected:

First, the communication must be maintained "on behalf of, and received by means of electronic transmission from (or created by means of computer processing of communications received by means of electronic transmission from), a subscriber or customer of such service. Second, the communication must be maintained, "solely for the purpose of providing storage or computer processing services to such subscriber or customer, if the provider is not authorized to access the contents of any such communications for purposes of providing any services other than storage or computer processing."

SCA levies fines and imprisonment for those who intentionally accesses without authorization a facility through which an electronic communication service is provided or intentionally exceeds an authorization to access that facility to alter, or prevent authorized access to a wire or electronic communication while it is in electronic storage.

Madrid Resolution[96]

In 2009, data protection authorities from 50 countries approved the "Madrid Resolution" on international minimums standards on of principles and rights to guarantee the effective protection of privacy at an international level. Data protection authorities from over 50 countries approve the "Madrid Resolution" on international privacy standards define a series of principles and rights

---

[96] (AEPD, 2009)

that guarantee the effective protection of privacy at an international level, as well as to ease the international flow of personal data, essential in a globalized world. Among the basic principles that must govern the use of personal data, and which have inspired the document, we find those of loyalty, legality, proportionality, quality, transparency and responsibility; the set of rights such as access, rectification, cancellation and objection and the way in which they can be exercised. It also includes obligations such as security of personal data, through those measures that are considered appropriate in each case, or confidentiality, which affects the controller as well as anyone who participates in any of the stages in which personal data is managed.

Family Educational Rights and Privacy Act (FERPA)[97]

The Family Educational Rights and Privacy Act (FERPA) is a Federal law that protects the privacy of student education records. The law applies to all schools that receive funds under an applicable program of the U.S. Department of Education. According to the law schools must have written permission from the parent or eligible student in order to release any information from a student's education record. However, FERPA allows schools to disclose those records, without consent in cases of health and safety emergencies. The consensus indicates that FERPA overrules HIPAA, in that individuals or their guardians/legal representatives must consent to the sharing of PHI, including health and educational records when both types of

[97] (2007b)

information are present. FERPA's legal foothold could reach could include:

1. Enhancement of immunization registries and linkage with other health records to produce Child Health Profiles (CHP)
2. Regional Health Information Organization (RHIO) demonstration projects to link together patient medical records
3. Insurance company projects linked to ICD-9 codes and patient records for cost-benefit assessments
4. Consortia of EHR developers collaborating to model systems requirements and standards for data linkage.

Federal Trade Commission Act (FTC)[98]

The FTC has been the chief federal agency on privacy policy and enforcement since the1970s, when it began enforcing one of the first federal privacy laws – the Fair Credit Reporting Act. Since then, rapid changes in technology have raised new privacy challenges, but the FTC's overall approach has been consistent: The agency uses law enforcement, policy initiatives, and consumer and business education to protect consumers' personal information and ensure that they have the confidence to take advantage of the many benefits of the ever-changing marketplace.

1. FTC's Privacy Report: Balancing Privacy and Innovation
2. The Do Not Track Option: Giving Consumers a Choice
3. Making Sure Companies Keep Their Privacy Promises to Consumers

---

[98] (2016b)

4. Protecting Consumers' Financial Privacy
5. The Children's Online Privacy Protection Act (COPPA): What Parents Should Know

Section 5 of the When companies tell consumers they will safeguard their personal information, the FTC can and does take law enforcement action to make sure that companies live up these promises. Federal Trade Commission Act prohibits "unfair or deceptive acts or practices in or affecting commerce." The prohibition applies to all persons engaged in commerce.

A health billing company and its former CEO have settled Federal Trade Commission charges they misled thousands of consumers who signed up for an online billing portal by failing to adequately inform them that the company would seek highly detailed medical information from pharmacies, medical labs and insurance companies.

The FTC charged that Payments made used the sign-up process for a "Patient Portal" -- where consumers could view their billing history -- as a pathway to deceptively seek consumers' consent to obtain detailed medical information about the consumers. The company and a third party began developing a separate service known as Patient Health Report, designed to provide consumers with comprehensive online medical records. In order to populate the medical records, though, the company first needed to acquire consumers' medical information. The complaints allege that the company altered the registration process for the billing portal to include permission for the company and its partners to contact healthcare providers to obtain their medical information.

Sarbanes-Oxley

The 2002 Sarbanes-Oxley Act (SOX) aims to ensure corporate accountability by requiring that organizations implement IT security controls within the corporate network. Network systems must ensure confidentiality, integrity, accuracy, of data.

SOX was passed to protect investors from the possibility of fraudulent accounting activities by corporations. Companies operating in the regulatory space are required to audit and validate their IT systems to ensure that their business processes and underlying records comply with regulations. The SOX Act mandated strict reforms to improve financial disclosures from corporations and prevent accounting fraud. Because business process are heavily dependent on IT for reporting business should establish and maintain internal controls and determine the effectiveness of their information management systems.

Health Information Technology for Economic and Clinical Health (HITECH)[99]

HITECH was signed into law on February 17, 2009, to promote the adoption and meaningful use of health information technology. HITECH addresses the privacy and security concerns associated with the electronic transmission of health information. HITECH lays out specific privacy and security rules, and defines whom the rules apply.

---

[99] (Health and Human Services, 2009)

The consequences of non-compliance are potentially severe, including both civil and criminal penalties. HITECH Extends the Scope and Penalties of HIPAA by addressing privacy and security concerns associated with the electronic transmission of health information. It strengthens the civil and criminal enforcement of the HIPAA rules by requiring that entities make public notification when data breaches occur. It stresses the needs for better controls surrounding.

1. Unique user identification track user identity
2. Emergency access procedure procedures for obtaining necessary electronic protected health information during an emergency.
3. Automatic logoff Implement electronic procedures that terminate an electronic session after a predetermined time of inactivity.
4. Encryption and decryption Implement a mechanism to encrypt and decrypt electronic protected health information.
5. Implement Audit controls mechanisms that record and examine activity in information systems that contain or use electronic protected health information.
6. Implement policies and procedures to protect electronic protected health information from improper alteration or destruction.
7. Implementation Mechanism to authenticate electronic protected health information (Addressable). Implement electronic mechanisms to corroborate that electronic protected health information has not been altered or destroyed in an unauthorized manner.
8. Implement procedures to verify that a person or entity seeking access to electronic protected health information is the one claimed.

9. Implement technical security measures to guard against unauthorized access

10. Implement security measures to ensure that electronically transmitted electronic protected health information is not improperly modified without detection until disposed of.

Gramm-Leach-Bliley[100]

The Gramm-Leach-Bliley Act requires financial institutions – companies that offer consumers financial products or services like loans, financial or investment advice, or insurance – to explain their information-sharing practices to their customers and to safeguard sensitive data. also known as the Financial Modernization Act of 1999, is a federal law enacted in the United States to control the ways that financial institutions deal with the private information of individuals. Companies that offer consumers financial products or services like loans, financial or investment advice, or insurance – to explain their information-sharing practices to their customers and to safeguard sensitive data.

This new law will require health plans and insurers to take a variety of actions with respect to the handling of member and subscriber data, in electronic and other formats, which parallel certain aspects of their HIPAA compliance efforts. In short, Information regarding medical condition or diagnosis must be kept separately from information used in employee assessment, on boarding, firing and promotions. Because HIPPA has regulatory jurisdiction over medical records, the risk associated with releasing medical information nay be

[100] (GPO,1914)

greater that personal information. Privacy vs. Security is a real dilemma.

21 CFR Part 11, Electronic Records; Electronic Signatures (ERES)

Part 11, Electronic Records; Electronic Signatures ERES applies to drug makers, medical device manufacturers, biotech companies, biologics developers, CROs, and other FDA-regulated industries. This document provides guidance to persons who, in fulfillment of a requirement maintain records, submit, or submit designated information electronically. As companies start to move from paper records to a digi-tal format, the need for security and privacy birthed Part 11. ERES applies to records in electronic form that are created, modified, maintained, archived, retrieved, or transmitted under any records requirements according to agency regulations. Agency enforcement includes but not limited to:

1. limiting system access to authorized individuals
2. use of operational system checks
3. Use of authority checks
4. Use of device checks
5. Determination that persons who develop, maintain, or use electronic systems have the
6. Education, training, and experience to perform their assigned tasks
7. Establishment of and adherence to written policies that hold individuals accountable for
8. Actions initiated under their electronic signatures
9. Appropriate controls over systems documentation

10. Controls for open systems corresponding to controls for closed systems bulleted above

Patriot Act[101]

The USA Patriot Act Provide Tools Required to Intercept and Obstruct Terrorism. The US government undue and unfettered access to their data if they choose to store it on the cloud servers of US providers. The major objective of the Patriot Act is "to deter and punish terrorist acts in the United States and around the world [and] to enhance law enforcement investigatory tools" by dramatically reducing restrictions pertaining to law enforcement requests to search telephone records, e-mail communication, and health records.

National Security and Intelligence Activities, public health departments, law enforcement agencies, federal agencies may disclose your health information to authorized officials who are conducting national security and intelligence activities or providing protective services to the President or other important officials.

The Patriot Act Give local law enforcement and the Federal Government powers to access medical information without a warrant. This include records from apply to many other organizations, including health plans, pharmacies, health clearinghouses, medical research facilities and various medical associations. This can be completed with only general notification and without specificity to the nature of the request.

---

[101] (GPO,2001)

Electronic Communications Privacy Act (ECPA)[102]

The Electronic Communications Privacy Act (ECPA) of 1986 specifies standards for government monitoring of cell phone conversations and Internet communications. Congress passed the Electronic Communications Privacy Act (ECPA) as a way to ensure that electronic communications were protected against wrongful use and public disclosure by third parties, including government agencies. The ECPA, as amended, protects wire, oral, and electronic communications while those communications are being made, are in transit, and when they are stored on computers. The Act applies to e-mail , telephone conversations, and data stored electronically.

The ECPA, which is called the Stored Communications Act (SCA), protects the privacy of the contents of files stored by service providers and of records held about the subscriber by service providers, such as subscriber name, billing records, or IP addresses. Some information can be obtained from providers with a subpoena; other information requires a special court order; and still other information requires a search warrant. ECPA outlaws the unauthorized interception of wire, oral, or electronic communications and establish a set of privacy requirements. The requirements include but not limited to:

1. Unlawful access to stored communications
2. Voluntary disclosure of customer communications or records

---

[102] (loc.gov,2006)

3. Required disclosure of customer communications or records
4. Backup preservation

ECPA also sets a path for government access to, stored electronic communications and establish procedures for government use of use of pen registers as well as trap and trace devices for use in law enforcement and foreign intelligence investigations.

Safe Harbor Agreement[103]

The European Commission's Directive on Data Protection went into effect in October of 1998, and would prohibit the transfer of personal data to non-European Union countries that do not meet the European Union (EU) "adequacy" standard for privacy protection. While the United States and the EU share the goal of enhancing privacy protection for their citizens, the United States takes a different approach

EU-U.S. cooperation over the trans-Atlantic digital economy fell apart in October 2015. The European Court of Justice (ECJ) struck down a critical data-sharing deal known as the Safe Harbor Agreement. This could had a serious effect on cloud hosting vendors and prove extremely disruptive to the world of compliance, and investigations. The ruling makes the more than five thousand companies whose self certify to conduct data transfers illegal. It is important to verify where your data is being stored.

---

[103] (Weiss, 2016)

Freedom of Information Act (FOIA)[104]

The Freedom The Freedom of Information Act (FOIA) is a law that gives persons the right to access information from the federal government. It is often described as the law that keeps citizens in the know about their government. Federal agencies are required to disclose records upon receipt of a written request, with some exceptions. This right of access is enforceable in court. The Freedom of Information Act (FOIA) provides public access to all federal agency records except for those records (or portions of those records) that are protected from disclosure. As part of the Bioresearch Monitoring Information System, HHS/FDA make the following databases for the below offices available for independent searches

1. Center for Biologics Evaluation and Research,
2. Center for Devices and Radiological Health
3. Center for Drug Evaluation and Research
4. Center for Food Safety and Applied Nutrition
5. Office of Regulatory Affairs
6. Center for Tobacco Products
7. Center for Veterinary Medicine

World Trade Organization (WTO)[105]

The World Trade Organization (WTO) is the only global international organization dealing with the rules of trade between nations. At its heart are the WTO agreements, negotiated and signed by the bulk of the world's trading nations and ratified in their

---

[104] (1996)
[105] (1996b)

parliaments. Their work includes ensuring that the regulations of each nation support the rights and obligations of WTO agreements. FDA incorporates these obligations into our regulatory process, specifically to ensure that our regulations are risk and science-based, are created through a transparent process, and are equitable to both domestic and foreign producers, while protecting public health.

WTO's General Agreement on Trade in Services Article XIV: General Exception (ii), the protection of the privacy of individuals in relation to the processing and dissemination of personal data and the protection of confidentiality of individual records and accounts;

> (ii) The protection of the privacy of individuals in relation to the processing and dissemination of personal data and the protection of confidentiality of individual records and accounts;

Free Trade Agreements

The United States has free trade agreements (FTAs) in force with 20 countries. The United States is Member of the World Trade Organization (WTO), and the Marrakesh Agreement. The World Trade Organization (WTO Agreement) sets out rules governing trade among the WTO's 154 members. The United States uses the FTA to strengthen consumer rights in the digital world. Consumer Privacy Bill of Rights will be implemented by the Federal Trade Commission which monitors compliance with data protection rules in the business sector.

1. Individual Control: Consumers have a right to exercise control over what personal data companies collect from them and how they use it.

2. Transparency: Consumers have a right to easily understandable and accessible information about privacy and security practices.
3. Respect for Context: Consumers have a right to expect that companies will collect, use, and disclose personal data in ways that are consistent with the context in which consumers provide the data.
4. Security: Consumers have a right to secure and responsible handling of personal data.
5. Access and Accuracy: Consumers have a right to access and correct personal data in usable formats, in a manner that is appropriate to the sensitivity of the data and the risk of adverse consequences to consumers if the data is inaccurate.
6. Focused Collection: Consumers have a right to reasonable limits on the personal data that companies collect and retain.
7. Accountability: Consumers have a right to have personal data handled by companies with appropriate measures in place to assure they adhere to the Consumer Privacy Bill of Rights.

Payment Card Industry Data Security Standard (PCI DSS)[106]

The Payment Card Industry Data Security Standard (PCI DSS) is a set of requirements designed to ensure that companies that process, store or transmit credit card information maintain a secure environment. PCI SSC has Data Security Standards. These requirements will help merchants and other organizations incrementally protect against the highest risk factors and escalating threats when transferring personal information.

---

[106] (PCI Security Standards Council, 2016)

Appendix A: Global Regulatory Authorities[107]

U.S. Food and Drug Administration

Multinational Organizations
World Health Organization
Pan-American Health Organization
WHO Regional Office for Europe
WHO Regional Office for Africa
WHO Regional Office for the Eastern Mediterranean
WHO Regional Office for Southeast Asia
WHO Regional Office for the Western Pacific
Food and Agriculture Organizations of the United Nations
Codex Alimentarius
World Trade Organization

Asia and the Pacific
Australian Government: Department of Health and Ageing
Australian Government: Therapeutic Goods Administration
Brunei: Ministry of Health
People's Republic of China: Ministry of Health (in Chinese)
People's Republic of China: State Food and Drug Administration (in Chinese)
People's Republic of China: National Institute for the Control of Pharmaceutical and Biological Products (in Chinese)
People's Republic of China: Ministry of Agriculture (in Chinese)
Fiji: Ministry of Health
Hong Kong: Department of Health
India: Ministry of Consumer Affairs, Food & Public Distribution
India: Central Drug Standards Control Organisation
India: Ministry of Food and Consumer Affairs
Indonesia: Ministry of Health (in Indonesian)
Japan: Ministry of Health, Labour and Welfare
Japan: Pharmaceuticals and Medical Devices Evaluation Agency
Japan: Ministry of Agriculture, Fisheries and Food (in Japanese)
Korea: Food and Drug Administration (in Korean)
Malaysia: Ministry of Health (in Malaysian)

---

[107] (2017a)

Appendix A: Global Regulatory Authorities

Malaysia: National Pharmaceutical Control Bureau (in Malaysian)
New Zealand: Ministry of Health
New Zealand: Medicines and Medical Devices Safety Authority
New Zealand: Food Safety Authority
Papua New Guinea: Department of Health
Philippines: Department of Health
Philippines: National Food Authority
Singapore: Ministry of Health
Singapore: Health Sciences Authority
Singapore: Ministry of Environment (food control)
Sri Lanka: Ministry of Health
Taiwan: Department of Health
Taiwan: National Laboratories of Foods and Drugs (in Chinese)
Thailand: Ministry of Public Health (in Thai)
Thailand: Food and Drug Administration
Thailand: Ministry of Agriculture and Co-operatives

Europe
European Medicines Agency (EMA)
European Commission Directorate General for Health & Consumers
European Commission Directorate General: Medicinal Products for Veterinary Use
European Commission Directorate General: Health Notice to Applicants
European Commission Consumer Affairs: Medical Devices
Andorra: Ministry of Health and Welfare (in Catalan)
Armenia: Ministry of Health (in Armenian)
Armenia: Drug and Medical Technology Agency (in Armenian)
Austria: Secretariat of Health (in German)
Belgium: Health, Food Chain Safety and Environment
Belgium: Pharmaceutical Inspectorate
Belgium: Federal Agency for the Safety of the Food Chain (in German)
Bulgaria: Ministry of Health (in Bulgarian)
Bulgaria: Drug Agency (in Bulgarian)
Croatia: Ministry of Health and Social Care
Czech Republic: Ministry of Health (in Czech)

Appendix A: Global Regulatory Authorities

Czech Republic: State Institute for Drug Control (in Czech)
Denmark: Ministry of Health
Danish Medicines Agency
Denmark: Ministry of Food, Agriculture and Fisheries
Denmark: Veterinary and Food Administration
Estonia: Ministry of Social Affairs
Estonia: State Agency of Medicines
Finland: Ministry of Social Affairs and Health
Finnish Medicines Agency
Finnish Food Safety Authority Evira
France: Ministry of Health (in French)
France: Sanitary Safety of Health Products Agency (in French)
France: National Agency for Veterinary Medicinal Products
Georgia: Ministry of Labor, Health and Social Affairs (in Arabic)
Georgia: Ministry of Agriculture (in Arabic)
Germany: Ministry of Health
Germany: Federal Institute for Drugs and Medical Devices
Germany: Robert Koch Institute (in German)
Germany: Paul Ehrlich Institute (in German)
Germany: Federal Institute for Risk Assessment (in German)
Germany: Ministry of Consumer Protection, Food and Agriculture (in German)
Greece: Ministry of Health and Social Solidarity (in Greek)
Greece: National Organization for Medicines
Greece: Hellenic Food Authority
Greece: Hellenic Ministry of Agriculture
Hungary: Ministry of Health, Social and Family Affairs (in Hungarian)
Hungary: National Institute of Pharmacy (in Hungarian)
Iceland: Ministry for Health and Social Security (In Icelandic)
Icelandic Medicines Agency (in Icelandic)
Iceland: The Environment Agency
Ireland: Department of Health and Children
Irish Medicines Board
Ireland: Food Safety Authority

Appendix A: Global Regulatory Authorities

Ireland: Agriculture and Food Development Authority
Italy: Ministry of Health (in Italian)
Italy: National Institute of Health (in Italian)
Latvia: State Agency of Medicines (in Latvian)
Lithuania: Ministry of Health
Lithuania: State Medicines Control Agency
Luxembourg: Ministry of Health (in French)
Luxembourg: Food Safety (in French)
Malta: Ministry of Health, Elderly and Community Care
Netherlands: Ministry of Health, Welfare and Sport
Netherlands: Medicines Evaluation Board (in Dutch)
Netherlands: Inspectorate for Health Protection and Veterinary Public Health (in Dutch)
Inspectie voor de Gezondheidszorg Ministere van Volksgezondheid, Welzjin en Sport (in Dutch)
Norway: Ministry of Health and Care Services
Norway: Norwegian Board of Health Supervision
Norway: Food Safety Authority (in Norwegian)
Norway: Norwegian Medicines Agency
Norway: Ministry of Agriculture and Food
Poland: Ministry of Health and Social Security (in Polish)
Poland: Drug Institute
Poland: Ministry of Agriculture and Rural Development (in Polish)
Portugal: Ministry of Health (in Portuguese)
Portugal: National Authority of Medicines and Health Products (in Portuguese)
Romania: Ministry of Health and the Family (in Romanian)
Russian Federation: Ministry of Public Health (in Russian)
San Marino, Ministry of Health and Social Security, National Insurance and Gender Equality (in Italian)
Slovak Republic: Ministry of Health (in Slovak)
Slovak Republic: State Institute for Drug Control (in Slovak)
Slovak Republic: Ministry of Agriculture and Rural Development
Slovak Republic: State Veterinary and Food Administration (in Slovak)
Slovenia: Ministry of Health (in Slovenian)

Appendix A: Global Regulatory Authorities

Slovenia: Institute of Public Health (in Slovenian)
Slovenia: Ministry of Agriculture, Forestry and Food
Spain: Ministry of Health and Consumption (in Spanish)
Spanish Agency for Medicines and Health Products (in Spanish)
Sweden: Medical Products Agency
Sweden: National Board of Health and Welfare (in Swedish)
Sweden: National Food Administration
Sweden: Ministry for Rural Affairs
Switzerland: Federal Office of Public Health
Switzerland: Agency for Therapeutic Products (in German)
Switzerland: Federal Veterinary Office
Switzerland: Federal Office for Agriculture (in German)
Turkey: Ministry of Health (in Turkish)
Ministry of Agriculture and Village Affairs (in Turkish)
Ukraine: Ministry of Health (in Ukrainian)
UK: Department of Health
UK: Health Protection Agency
UK: Medicines and Healthcare Products Regulatory Agency
UK: National Institute for Biological Standards and Control
UK: Food Standards Agency
UK: Veterinary Medicines Directorate

Middle East
Bahrain: Ministry of Health (in Arabic)
Israel: Ministry of Health
Israel: Ministry of Industry, Trade and Labor
Jordan: Ministry of Health
Lebanon: Ministry of Public Health
Palestinian Authority: Ministry of Health (in Arabic)
Saudi Arabia: Ministry of Health
United Arab Emirates: Ministry of Health
United Arab Emirates: Federal Department of Pharmacies
Yemen: Ministry of Public Health & Population

Appendix A: Global Regulatory Authorities

Africa
Benin: Ministry of Health (in French)
Botswana: Ministry of Health
Egypt: Ministry of Agriculture and Land Reclamation
Ghana: Ministry of Health
Ghana: Ministry of Food and Agriculture
Kenya: Ministry of Health
Maldives: Ministry of Health
Mauritius: Ministry of Health & Quality of Life
Mauritius: Ministry of Agro Industry and Food Security
Morocco: Ministry of Public Health (in French)
Namibia: Ministry of Health and Social Services
Namibia: Ministry of Fisheries and Marine Resources
Senegal: Ministry of Health and Prevention (in French)
South Africa: Department of Health
Swaziland: Ministry of Health and Social Welfare
Tanzania: Ministry of Health
Tunisia: Ministry of Public Health (in French)
Tunisia: Office of Pharmacy and Medicines (in French)
Uganda: Ministry of Health
Zimbabwe: Ministry of Health and Child Welfare

South America
Argentina: Ministry of Health (in Spanish)
Argentina: National Administration of Drugs, Foods and Medical Technology (in Spanish)
Belize: Ministry of Health
Bolivia: Ministry of Health and Social Welfare
Brazil: Ministry of Health (in Portuguese)
Brazil: National Health Surveillance Agency (in Portuguese)
Brazil: Fundacao Oswaldo Cruz
Canada: Health Products and Food Branch
Canada: Food Inspection Agency
Chile: Health Ministry (in Spanish)
Chile: Institute of Public Health (in Spanish)
Colombia: Ministry of Health (in Spanish)

Appendix A: Global Regulatory Authorities

Colombia: INVIMA Instituto Nacional de Vigilancia de Medicamentos y Alimentos (in Spanish)
Costa Rica: Ministry of Health (in Spanish)
Dominican Republic: Ministry of Agriculture (in Spanish)
Ecuador: Ministry of Public Health (in Spanish)
El Salvador: Ministry of Public Health and Social Assistance (in Spanish)
El Salvador: Ministry of Agriculture (in Spanish)
Guatemala: Ministry of Health (in Spanish)
Guyana: Ministry of Health
Guyana: National Bureau of Standards
Jamaica: Ministry of Health
Mexico: Ministry of Health (in Spanish)
Mexico: Federal Commission for the Protection Against Sanitary Risks
Netherlands Antilles: Department of Public Health and Environmental Protection
Nicaragua: Ministry of Health (in Spanish)
Panama: Ministry of Health (in Spanish)
Peru: Ministry of Health (in Spanish)
Peru: General Directorate of Medicines, Supplies and Drugs (in Spanish)
St. Lucia: Ministry of Agriculture, Lands Forestry and Fisheries
Trinidad and Tobago: Ministry of Health
Trinidad & Tobago: Bureau of Standards
Uruguay: Ministry of Public Health (in Spanish)
Venezuela: Ministry of Health and Social Development (in Spanish)

Bibliography

1. Matloff, N. (2015) Parallel computing for data science: With examples in R, C++ and Cuda. Boca Raton, FL, United States: CRC Press.
2. Joseph, J., Fellenstein, C. and Moss, G.L. (2003) Grid computing. United States: Prentice Hall.
3. Lutchman, R. (2003) Computerized work management systems for utility and plant operations. Lancaster, PA: DEStech Publications.
4. Metheny, M. (2013) Federal cloud computing: The definitive guide for cloud service providers. New York, NY, United States: Syngress Publishing.
5. EXHIBIT 300 CAPITAL ASSET PLAN AND BUSINESS CASE SUMMARY (no date) Available at: https://www.gsa.gov/graphics/staffoffices/300ioi.pdf (Accessed: 8 December 2016).
6. Schlosser, L., Member, B., Peter Tseronis, DOE, Peter Mell, NIST and for ISPAB (2009) Federal cloud computing governance framework. Available at: http://csrc.nist.gov/groups/SMA/ispab/documents/minutes/2009-12/cloud-computing-government-tic.pdf (Accessed: 8 December 2016).
7. S. Rept. 113-157 - THE FEDERAL DATA CENTER CONSOLIDATION ACT OF 2013 (no date) Available at: https://www.congress.gov/congressional-report/113th-congress/senate-report/157/1 (Accessed: 8 December 2016).
8. KellyJOlson (2011) Available at: https://www.gsa.gov/graphics/staffoffices/FY2011OCSITAnnualReport.pdf (Accessed: 8 December 2016).
9. Program overview (no date) Available at: https://www.fedramp.gov/about-us/about/ (Accessed: 8 December 2016).
10. Department of Homeland Security, Office of the Chief Procurement Officer (2015) Security authorization process guide version 11.1. Available at:

https://www.dhs.gov/sites/default/files/publications/Security%20 Authorization%20Process%20Guide_v11_1.pdf (Accessed: 8 December 2016).

11. Hawes, K. (2016) What ITL does. Available at: https://www.nist.gov/itl/about-itl (Accessed: 8 December 2016).

12. Mell, P. and Grance, T. (2012) The NIST definition of cloud computing recommendations of the national institute of standards and technology special publication 800-145. Available at: http://nvlpubs.nist.gov/nistpubs/Legacy/SP/nistspecialpublication 800-145.pdf (Accessed: 8 December 2016).

13. FDA (2015) Information technology strategic plan 2015-2018. Available at: http://www.fda.gov/downloads/AboutFDA/ReportsManualsForm s/Reports/UCM325437.pdf (Accessed: 8 December 2016).

14. |, E., Ferraro, F. and Carmona, J. (2015) IN-DEPTH ANALYSIS. Available at: http://www.europarl.europa.eu/RegData/etudes/IDAN/2015/554 168/EPRS_IDA(2015)554168_EN.pdf (Accessed: 8 December 2016).

15. Metheny, M. (2013) Federal cloud computing: The definitive guide for cloud service providers. New York, NY, United States: Syngress Publishing.

16. COMM, 2016a)

17. COMM, 2016b)

18. COMM, 2012)

19. (Schlosser et al., 2009)

20. YOUR RIGHTS AS A DATA SUBJECT WHAT CAN YOU DO IF YOUR RIGHTS ARE VIOLATED DATA TRANSFERS TO NON-EU COUNTRIES USEFUL ADDRESSES AND NUMBERS (no date) Available at: http://ec.europa.eu/justice/policies/privacy/docs/guide/guide-ukingdom_en.pdf (Accessed: 8 December 2016).

21. |, E., Ferraro, F. and Carmona, J. (2015) IN-DEPTH ANALYSIS. Available at: http://www.europarl.europa.eu/RegData/etudes/IDAN/2015/554

168/EPRS_IDA(2015)554168_EN.pdf (Accessed: 8 December 2016).

22. (COMM, 2017)
23. (European, no date)
24. Sekaran, C.K. (2014) Essentials of cloud computing. Canada: Apple Academic Press.
25. Jones, M.L. (2016) Ctrl + Z: The right to be forgotten. United States: New York University Press.
26. Olson, J.E. and White, C. (2002) Data quality: The accuracy dimension. San Francisco: Elsevier Science.
27. Stalla-Bourdillon, S., Phillips, J. and Ryan, M.D. (2014a) Privacy vs. Security. United Kingdom: Springer London.
28. Snedaker, S. and Rogers, R. (2006) Syngress IT security project management handbook. United States: Syngress Media,U.S.
29. McDowall, R.D. (2002) 'The impact of 21 CFR 11 (electronic records and electronic signatures final rule) on bioanalysis', Chromatographia, 55(S1), pp. S85–S90. doi: 10.1007/bf02493360.
30. Green, S. and Millstein, I.M. (2004) Manager's guide to the Sarbanes-Oxley act: Improving internal controls to prevent fraud. New York, NY, United States: Wiley, John & Sons.
31. Santoro, G., Robin, F. and Administration, D. (2002) Compact Regs Cfr 21 part 11: Part 11, electronic records; electronic signatures (10-Pack). Boca Raton, FL, United States: CRC Press.
32. Guidance for industry process validation: General principles and practices (2011) Available at: http://www.fda.gov/downloads/Drugs/Guidances/UCM070336.pdf (Accessed: 24 January 2017).
33. Center and Health, R. (2016) Quality system (QS) regulation. Available at: http://www.fda.gov/medicaldevices/deviceregulationandguidance/postmarketrequirements/qualitysystemsregulations/ (Accessed: 24 January 2017).

34. Sulfanilamide disaster (2015) Available at: http://www.fda.gov/AboutFDA/WhatWeDo/History/ProductRegulation/SulfanilamideDisaster/ucm2007257.htm (Accessed: 10 February 2017).

35. Center, Health, R. and Evaluation, B. (2016) Guidance for the content of Premarket submissions for software contained in medical devices. Available at: http://www.fda.gov/MedicalDevices/DeviceRegulationandGuidance/GuidanceDocuments/ucm089543.htm (Accessed: 10 February 2017).

36. Dent, N. (ed.) (1996) Good research practices: A practical guide to the implementation of the GXP's. Oxford: Butterworth-Heinemann.

37. Bendebka, R. and Hossain, I. (2012) The Asia-Pacific economic cooperation (Apec). Germany: LAP Lambert Academic Publishing.

38. CPDCS_PGV1 (no date) CPDCS PGV1. Available at: http://www.aseanconsumer.org/accp/uploads/files/CPDCS_PGV1.pdf (Accessed: 12 February 2017).

39. Al-Mubaraki, H., Al-Ajmei, R., Ahmed, A., Sciences and Research, T.P. (2013) Best practices of business Incubators in developed and developing countries: The Roadmap for the gulf cooperation council (GCC) countries. Brighton: World Association for Sustainable Development (WASD).

40. Mitchell, C. (2016) PAHO WHO | about the PANDRH network. Available at: http://www.paho.org/hq/index.php?option=com_content&view=article&id=11818%3Aacerca-de-la-red-parf&catid=8594%3Aacerca-de&Itemid=41774&lang=en (Accessed: 10 February 2017).

41. Muntschick, J. (2017) The southern African development community (SADC) and the European Union (EU): Regionalism and external influence. Switzerland: Springer International Publishing AG.

42. Mentions, I.L. (2017) ICH official web site: ICH. Available at: http://www.ich.org/home.html (Accessed: 10 February 2017).

43. AS ISO 15489 Australian standard on records management (2017) Available at: http://prov.vic.gov.au/government/standards-and-policy/all-documents/as-iso-15489 (Accessed: 10 February 2017).

44. Institution, B.S. and Institute, B.S. (2001) BS ISO 15489-1: 2001 information and documentation: Records management. London: BSI Standards.

45. Guidance for industry part 11, electronic records; electronic signatures — scope and application (2003) Available at: http://www.fda.gov/downloads/RegulatoryInformation/Guidances/ucm125125.pdf (Accessed: 10 February 2017).

46. CFR 2011 title21 vol4 part211 (2014) Available at: https://www.gpo.gov/fdsys/pkg/CFR-2011-title21-vol4/pdf/CFR-2011-title21-vol4-part211.pdf (Accessed: 10 February 2017).

47. Commissioner, O. of the (2014) Bioterrorism act of 2002. Available at: http://www.fda.gov/regulatoryinformation/legislation/ucm148797.htm (Accessed: 10 February 2017).

48. Commissioner, O. of the (2016) Federal food, drug, and cosmetic act (FD&C act). Available at: http://www.fda.gov/regulatoryinformation/legislation/federalfooddrugandcosmeticactfdcact/ (Accessed: 10 February 2017).

49. carolyn.becker (2006) GUIDANCE FOR INDUSTRY prescription drug marketing act (PDMA) requirements Available at: http://www.fda.gov/downloads/drugs/guidancecomplianceregulatoryinformation/guidances/ucm134399.pdf (Accessed: 10 February 2017).

50. Commissioner, O. of the (2015) Food and drug administration amendments act (FDAAA) of 2007. Available at: http://www.fda.gov/RegulatoryInformation/Legislation/SignificantAmendmentstotheFDCAct/FoodandDrugAdministrationAmendmentsActof2007/default.htm (Accessed: 10 February 2017).

51. Commissioner, O. of the (2016b) Food and drug administration safety and innovation act (FDASIA). Available at: http://www.fda.gov/RegulatoryInformation/Legislation/SignificantAmendmentstotheFDCAct/FDASIA/ucm20027187.htm (Accessed: 10 February 2017).

52. Center, Safety, F. and Nutrition, A. (2017) Subscribe. Available at: http://www.fda.gov/Food/GuidanceRegulation/FSMA/ (Accessed: 10 February 2017).

53. Center, Safety, F. and Nutrition, A. (2015) Current good manufacturing practices (CGMPs). Available at: http://www.fda.gov/food/guidanceregulation/cgmp/

54. Center and Evaluation, B. (2015) Rules, Guidances & recommendations. Available at: http://www.fda.gov/BiologicsBloodVaccines/GuidanceComplianceRegulatoryInformation/ (Accessed: 10 February 2017).

55. Center and Health, R. (2016) Additional information. Available at: http://www.fda.gov/MedicalDevices/DeviceRegulationandGuidance/Overview/ (Accessed: 10 February 2017).

56. PLAW 113publ54 (2013) Available at: https://www.gpo.gov/fdsys/pkg/PLAW-113publ54/pdf/PLAW-113publ54.pdf (Accessed: 10 February 2017).

57. USCODE 2011 title28 partV chap115 sec1732 (2012) Available at: https://www.gpo.gov/fdsys/pkg/USCODE-2011-title28/pdf/USCODE-2011-title28-partV-chap115-sec1732.pdf (Accessed: 10 February 2017).

58. Brumfield, P., Gregory, B.M., Mazurek, J.P., Beard, B.D., Beattie, R.C. and Miller, F.H. (2000) UNIFORM ELECTRONIC TRANSACTIONS ACT (1999) NATIONAL CONFERENCE OF COMMISSIONERS ON UNIFORM STATE LAWS and by it APPROVED AND RECOMMENDED FOR ENACTMENT IN ALL THE STATES at its. Available at: http://www.uniformlaws.org/shared/docs/electronic%20transactions/ueta_final_99.pdf (Accessed: 10 February 2017).

59. Karen.Stutsman (2004) Application integrity policy. Available at: http://www.fda.gov/downloads/ICECI/EnforcementActions/ApplicationIntegrityPolicy/ucm072631.pdf (Accessed: 10 February 2017).

60. ELECTRONIC SIGNATURES IN GLOBAL AND NATIONAL COMMERCE ACT (1910) Available at: https://www.gpo.gov/fdsys/pkg/PLAW-106publ229/pdf/PLAW-106publ229.pdf (Accessed: 10 February 2017).

61. Ltd, M.L.P. (2016) Federal rules of civil procedure; 2017 edition. United States: Michigan Legal Publishing.

62. Puglia, S., Reed, J., Rhodes, E., Chapman, S., Comstock, B., Hale, M. and David (2014) U.S. National archives and records administration (NARA) technical guidelines for Digitizing archival materials for electronic access: Creation of production master files – Raster images for the following record types-textual, graphic illustrations/Artwor. Available at: https://www.archives.gov/files/preservation/technical/guidelines.pdf (Accessed: 10 February 2017).

63. STATUTE 77 Pg630 (no date) Available at: https://www.gpo.gov/fdsys/pkg/STATUTE-77/pdf/STATUTE-77-Pg630.pdf (Accessed: 10 February 2017).

64. 805 ILCS 410/ uniform preservation of private business records act (2003) Available at: http://www.ilga.gov/legislation/ilcs/ilcs3.asp?ActID=2300&ChapterID=65 (Accessed: 10 February 2017).

65. Sarbanes-Oxley act of 2002 2004, c. Available at: https://www.sec.gov/about/laws/soa2002.pdf (Accessed: 10 February 2017).

66. Summary of the HIPAA privacy rule (2013) Available at: https://www.hhs.gov/hipaa/for-professionals/privacy/laws-regulations (Accessed: 10 February 2017).

67. FISMA final (no date) Available at: http://csrc.nist.gov/drivers/documents/FISMA-final.pdf (Accessed: 11 February 2017).

68. PLAW 106publ102 (1914) Available at: https://www.gpo.gov/fdsys/pkg/PLAW-106publ102/pdf/PLAW-106publ102.pdf (Accessed: 11 February 2017).

69. United States code, 2010 edition title 18 -CRIMES AND CRIMINAL PROCEDURE PART I -CRIMES CHAPTER 121 -STORED WIRE AND ELECTRONIC COMMUNICATIONS AND TRANSACTIONAL RECORDS ACCESS (2010) Available at: http://stanford.edu/~jmayer/law696/week6/Stored%20Communications%20Act.pdf (Accessed: 11 February 2017).

70. AIUM (2017) Available at: http://www.aium.org/ (Accessed: 11 February 2017).

71. ANSI-American national standards institute (2017) Available at: https://www.ansi.org/default (Accessed: 11 February 2017).

72. 28152796, A.S. of (2017a) Meeting information. Available at: http://acousticalsociety.org/ (Accessed: 11 February 2017).

73. The American society of mechanical engineers (2017) Available at: https://www.asme.org/ (Accessed: 11 February 2017).

74. ASTM, 2014 (1996) ASTM international - standards worldwide. Available at: https://www.astm.org/ (Accessed: 11 February 2017).

75. Home (2017) Available at: https://www.cen.eu/Pages/default.aspx (Accessed: 11 February 2017).

76. (cganet Accessed: 11 February 2017) Available at: http://www.cganet.com/ (Accessed: 11 February 2017).

77. Clinical and Institute, L.S. (no date) Clinical & laboratory standards institute: CLSI guidelines. Available at: http://clsi.org/ (Accessed: 11 February 2017).

78. Welcome to the IEC - international Electrotechnical commission (2016) Available at: http://www.iec.ch/ (Accessed: 11 February 2017).

79. IEEE (2017) Available at: https://www.ieee.org/index.html (Accessed: 11 February 2017).

80. Iso (2017) Enhancing traceability with a new ISO project committee. Available at: http://www.iso.org/iso/home.html (Accessed: 11 February 2017).

81. NEMA (2016) The association of electrical equipment and medical imaging manufacturers. Available at: http://www.nema.org/pages/default.aspx (Accessed: 11 February 2017).

82. NFPA (2016) NFPA. Available at: http://www.nfpa.org/ (Accessed: 11 February 2017).

83. RESNA (2016) Welcome to RESNA. Available at: http://www.resna.org/ (Accessed: 11 February 2017).

84. Superuser (2010) Illuminating engineering society. Available at: http://www.ies.org/ (Accessed: 11 February 2017).

85. UL (2017) UL. Available at: http://www.ul.com/ (Accessed: 11 February 2017).

86. Standards updates (2017) Standards updates. Available at: http://www.usp.org/ (Accessed: 11 February 2017).

87. International, A.S. (2016) AOAC member Login. Available at: https://www.aoac.org/AOAC_Prod_Imis/AOAC_Member/Default.aspx?WebsiteKey=2e25ab5a-1f6d-4d78-a498-19b9763d11b4&hkey=8fc2171a-6051-4e64-a928-5c47dfa25797 (Accessed: 11 February 2017).

88. Sciences, N.A. of (2016) Where the nation turns for independent, expert advice. Available at: http://www.nationalacademies.org/nasem/ (Accessed: 11 February 2017).

89. Krause, K., Amgen, San, I., Bay, F. / and Meeting, A.C. (2004) Good automated manufacturing practices (GAMP) ISPE/GAMP Americas steering committee. Available at: https://www.ispe.org/san-francisco/good-automated-manufacturing-practices-gamp.pdf (Accessed: 11 February 2017).

90. ANSI (2007) ANSI/AAMI/ISO 14971: 2007/(R)2010, medical devices - application of risk management to medical devices. Available at: http://my.aami.org/aamiresources/previewfiles/149711010_preview.pdf (Accessed: 11 February 2017).

91. ISPE and ISPE (2017) International society for pharmaceutical engineering. Available at: http://www.ispe.org/ (Accessed: 11 February 2017).

92. HHS (2013) Enforcement rule. Available at: https://www.hhs.gov/hipaa/for-professionals/special-topics/enforcement-rule/index.html (Accessed: 12 February 2017).

93. EUR-Lex (1995) Access to European Union law EUR-Lex Access to European Union law. Available at: http://eur-lex.europa.eu/legal-

content/en/TXT/?uri=CELEX%3A31995L0046 (Accessed: 12 February 2017).

94. PIPEDA (2016) PIPEDA compliance help - office of the privacy commissioner of Canada. Available at: https://www.priv.gc.ca/en/privacy-topics/privacy-laws-in-canada/the-personal-information-protection-and-electronic-documents-act-pipeda/pipeda-compliance-help/ (Accessed: 12 February 2017).

95. US Government Printing Office (2010) U.S.C. Title 18 - CRIMES AND CRIMINAL PROCEDURE. Available at: https://www.gpo.gov/fdsys/pkg/USCODE-2010-title18/html/USCODE-2010-title18-partI-chap121.htm (Accessed: 12 February 2017).

96. AEPD (2009) At the closed meeting of data protection authorities, within the 31 st international conference of data protection and privacy data protection authorities from over 50 countries approve the ' Madrid resolution ' on international privacy standards. Available at: http://www.privacyconference2009.org/media/notas_prensa/common/pdfs/061109_estandares_internacionales_en.pdf (Accessed: 12 February 2017).

97. US Department of Education U. S. Department of Education (2007b) Family educational rights and privacy act (FERPA). Available at: https://www2.ed.gov/policy/gen/guid/fpco/ferpa/index.html?src=rn (Accessed: 12 February 2017).

98. federalreserve (2016b) Federal trade commission act section 5: Unfair or deceptive acts or practices. Available at: https://www.federalreserve.gov/boarddocs/supmanual/cch/ftca.pdf (Accessed: 12 February 2017).

99. Health and Human Services (2009) Enforcement Interim Final Rule. Available at: https://www.hhs.gov/sites/default/files/ocr/privacy/hipaa/administrative/enforcementrule/enfifr.pdf?language=es (Accessed: 12 February 2017).

100. GPO (1914) PLAW 106publ102. Available at: https://www.gpo.gov/fdsys/pkg/PLAW-106publ102/pdf/PLAW-106publ102.pdf (Accessed: 12 February 2017).

101. GPO (2001) BILLS 107hr3162enr. Available at: https://www.gpo.gov/fdsys/pkg/BILLS-107hr3162enr/pdf/BILLS-107hr3162enr.pdf (Accessed: 12 February 2017).

102. loc.gov (2006) ElectronicCommunicationsPrivacyAct PL199 508. Available at: https://www.loc.gov/law/opportunities/PDFs/ElectronicCommunicationsPrivacyAct-PL199-508.pdf (Accessed: 12 February 2017).

103. Weiss, M.A. (2016) U.S.-EU data privacy: From safe harbor to privacy shield. Available at: https://fas.org/sgp/crs/misc/R44257.pdf (Accessed: 12 February 2017).

104. Department of Justice (1996) FOIA update: The freedom of information act, 5 U.S.C. Sect. 552, as amended by public law no. 104-231, 110 stat. 3048. Available at: https://www.justice.gov/oip/blog/foia-update-freedom-information-act-5-usc-sect-552-amended-public-law-no-104-231-110-stat (Accessed: 12 February 2017).

105. WTO (1996b) Rules of conduct. Available at: https://www.wto.org/english/tratop_e/dispu_e/rc_e.htm (Accessed: 12 February 2017).

106. PCI Security Standards Council (2016) PCI DSS Prioritized approach for PCI DSS 3.2 the Prioritized approach to pursue PCI DSS compliance. Available at: https://www.pcisecuritystandards.org/documents/Prioritized-Approach-for-PCI_DSS-v3_2.pdf?agreement=true&time=1487444651544 (Accessed: 18 February 2017).

107. PDA (2017a) Global regulatory authority Websites. Available at: https://www.pda.org/scientific-and-regulatory-affairs/regulatory-resources/global-regulatory-authority-websites#americas (Accessed: 11 February 2017).

Author Bio

Darral Addison is a regulatory professional who believes in a risk-based top down approach towards regulatory policy and enforcement and a bottoms up approach for its assimilation and integration. Darral has had the opportunity to accumulate over 40 years experience in the Clinical, Pharmaceutical, Biotech, Medical Device, Food and IT industries. He has held consulting positions for the world's top pharmaceutical and IT companies. He engages in large and small initiatives with regulatory-driven approaches, methodologies, and processes across all organizational levels.

Companies include: Verizon/Terremark, Gsk Pharmaceuticals, Shire Pharmaceuticals, Church & Dwight:, Astellas Biotechnology, Celgene Pharmaceuticals, Depuy Synthes, Mcneil, Hospira, Shin Nippon Biomedical Laboratories, Loma Linda University, Lannett Pharmaceuticals, Novartis/Ciba , Accenture, Pfizer Johnson & Johnson, Pfizer, Teleflex Medical, Illumina, Ge Healthcare Advanced Automation Centocor, Boston Scientific, Covance Alcon Pharmaceuticals, Cardinal Health, Omnicare Pharmaceuticals Astra-Zeneca, Whitehall-Robins Lanett Pharmaceuticals, and Rohm & Hass.

He has also worked in global various consulting positions

Positions include: Global Risk & Compliance (GRC), Global CSV Lead, Sr. QA Lead, Sr. Project Manager, Quality System Expert, (SME) Cleaning Validation, Sr. QA CD GMP Specialist, IT GMP Cloud Expert, Sr. Auditor, Sr. Validation Manager, Clinical System Project Manager, Laboratory Program Manager, Global Clinical Operations Manager, Quality Medical Device Project Validation Manager Sr. Software Quality Project Manager, Sr. Project Validation Manager IT-QA, QA, Process Control Validation Engineer, Global Remediation Technical Lead, QA Validation Consultant, Sr. Quality Assurance/Scientist, and Pharmaceutical Development Chemist

His professional credentials include: Masters in Quality Assurance/Regulatory Affairs, Graduate from the school of Pharmacy, Masters in Theology, Drug Development Temple University, and BA Chemistry

Written three books:

1. US and EU Cloud Computing Policy and Acceptance
2. Laws, Regulations and Standards Governing Personal, Private and Confidential Information Stored in Cloud and Personal Computers
3. How to Protect Personal, Private and Regulated Information in Cloud Systems and Personal Computers

Darral owns three companies:

1. **www.validatedqualitysystems.com** – Validated Quality Systems: Validated Quality System is a registered corporation. Validated Quality System (VQS) provides Validation and Quality System services.
2. **www.vqsstaffing.com** - Validated Quality Systems Staffing: VQS Staffing is a staff augmentation and consulting service.
3. **www.sionaddtechnologies.com** - Sionadd Technologies: Sionadd Technologies is a registered corporation. It is a one-stop hardware and software solutions leader in incorporating environmental detection and monitoring, data acquisition, programmable real-time data security and power management into our Programmable Remote Power Controllers.

Community

Darral is in the process building an accredited institution for teaching theology. He has visited hospitals in Eastern Africa to assess critical systems and their ability to provide meaningful services.

www.ingramcontent.com/pod-product-compliance
Lightning Source LLC
La Vergne TN
LVHW080041210926
848481LV00011B/3252
* 9 7 8 0 9 9 8 5 0 4 0 2 5 *